D0685154

# rock talk

# rock talk

## the great
## rock and roll
## quote
## book

Edited by

Joe Kohut and John J. Kohut

Faber and Faber
BOSTON • LONDON

All rights reserved under International and Pan-American Copyright
Conventions, including the right of reproduction in whole or in part in
any form. First published in 1994 in the United States by
Faber and Faber, Inc., 50 Cross Street, Winchester, MA 01890.

A CIP record for this book is available from the Library of Congress.

ISBN 0-571-19839-2

Cover design by Lorna Stovall
Printed in the United States of America

# contents

# acknowledgments

Thanks to D. U. Smith III for his support and endless
supply of goodwill and bourbon, Gary "The Dutch Boy"
Schaeffer for the clips, Charles Carr for his historical
sources, Roland Sweet for the right quote at the right
time, Sue Johnson for the best quotes we couldn't find,
MJ Walker for liking Lou Reed, and Louis Gribaudo and
the rest of the Leisure Kings (Philadelphia's best unsigned
band) for their early encouragement.

Many thanks to our editor Betsy Uhrig and her assistant
Suzanne Summers for making this an enjoyable
experience. They move like the wind.

Thanks also to our agent Gail Ross for her persistance.

Special thanks to all the rock and roll reporters who asked
the right questions in the first place.

And special thanks to Mom for making those cool vests
for us to wear at Woodstock and for never asking us to
"turn it down!"

# introduction

If Frederick Exley hadn't already put the title to good use nearly twenty-five years ago we might have called this introduction "A Fan's Notes" because first and foremost we are fans. Yes, indeed. Our blood runs a bit hotter and our eyes get a bit wider when we hear "a Telecaster through a Vibrolux turned up to ten." We firmly believe that "Zigaboo" Modeliste and all of Gene Krupa's other bastard children have successfully proven what physics can't: that the universe really does run on 4/4 time with a serious serving of fatback on the side.

While we are most at ease in a crowded, smoky bar listening to a no-name band that's just a little too loud, we have upon occasion gladly joined the herd in concrete tents built for contact sports to hear Bruce Springsteen conjure Rosalita's ghost while careening across the stage, and to see Keith Richards insinuate an entire lexicon of rhythm with just a sigh and a shrug of his shoulders.

We know in our hearts that the world would be a more interesting place if the real Clinton/Gore ticket had won: George Clinton and Lesley Gore. We have found salvation in the pocket of a bass line, the beatitudes in a backbeat. We are fans simply because even when nothing else in this world has made sense, the music always has. We also know that the music is more than that.

Rock and roll is a product. When we asked our favorite freelance bon vivant, D. U. Smith III, what he thought most rock and roll songs were about, his reply, which took all of a Manhattan heartbeat, was, "Most rock and roll songs are about three and a half minutes." Ever the realist, Smith's observation on the rule of radio play is an apt description of an industry that is designed to package the sublime and serve it up in manageable doses to adolescents and those of us who never completely left adolescence behind. The rock and roll business eats its old and wounded quicker than a Chilean rugby team. It's an industry where both the art and the artist are completely disposable, come stamped with their projected shelf life on the side, and are later recycled as commercials for home care products.

As a pair of former altar boys, we find that these apparent contradictions between art and dreams on the one hand and commerce on the other haven't made us any more cynical. On the contrary, we remain constantly amazed that the magic still continues to work as effectively as it does. Yeah, we're fans.

Having spent some time plying different parts of the journalist's trade, either dissecting the news or reporting it, we know that the most interesting stories are rarely left lying around on the front page. They're usually buried somewhere on page thirteen under the ads for crock pots, clock radios, and interest rates. So we decided to comb the back pages of close to forty years of newspapers, books, magazines, fanzines, videotapes, and the like for what we consider the gems that best explain, describe, and illuminate the world of rock and roll; a backstage pass carved from the observations and opinions of the people who make the music and do the business of the industry that has helped to shape the cultural context of contemporary life.

For good measure we have tossed a lot of extras into this rock and roll stew, including comments from the fans who made it all possible, the agents who cut the deals, the critics who tried to convince us that they knew what it really meant, and from that unwashed cultural minority among us who just never got with the program. They know who they are.

We admit from the gate that we are extremely catholic in our use of the term rock and roll. No one could accuse us of hardening of the categories. We've included the wisdom of wags from the worlds of "pop," "funk," "punk," "R&B," "country," "rockabilly," "blues," "hip-hop," and just about any other kind of contemporary popular music that stirred our souls and made us feel like it was Christmas, payday, and Saturday night all rolled into one.

Besides, if you're the kind of person that takes those artificial distinctions about music seriously you probably thought that Hall and Oates were too black for white radio and too white for black radio. Dante had a special place for people like you.

If after you've finished reading this volume you start screaming, "How could they leave out . . . ," just write to us and we promise to consider it for inclusion in the future. 'Til next time, remember to "TURN IT UP!" More bass, more drums, more guitars!!

Joe and John Kohut
Philadelphia, November 1993

# rock talk

# the business

I consider it my patriotic duty to keep Elvis in the ninety percent tax bracket.

*Colonel Tom Parker, upon Elvis Presley's*
*departure for the army*

You've got to be able to laugh at yourself in this business because there are so many bullshitters and wankers that fill
your head so full of shit that you don't know who you are.
That's why so many bands fuck up. They start believing what
people say about them and get big heads. I mean, at the end
of the day I'm just some snotty little kid from Stourbridge
who got lucky.

*Alex Griffin, Ned's Atomic Dustbin*

The music industry doesn't give the singer any control. Look
at Elvis Presley. He was the most successful, right? He died
kissing the place where the urine drips down the toilet, filled
with reds. His lip just hung up right there on the porcelain.
I'd say something was going wrong there.

*Phil Alvin, the Blasters*

During the session, Ringo turned to me and said, "I certainly
would like to record some of your songs." I'll be truthful with
you. Right between his eyes on that famous nose I saw the

prettiest dollar sign I had ever seen in my life. I said, "Help yourself, son. The whole catalog's yours."

*Carl Perkins*

There are guys that have had Top Ten hits that are fry cooks right now. They're in prison, or they're digging ditches, or they're living with their mom somewhere. It happens. You don't ever want to get overly confident in this business. The guys in Canned Heat—they had several Top Ten hits.

*Mike Mills, R.E.M.*

Get a good lawyer. And detach the person from the persona.
*Mickey Dolenz, the Monkees, giving advice to those*
*who reach superstardom*

I've seen too many of these old guys walk up at the Rock and Roll Hall of Fame and not even have a decent suit to wear and they get a trophy that costs $10.98, and you have the record company biggies standing there bragging about how little they paid these guys, and they laugh, and they think it's funny. That ain't gonna happen to me.

*Billy Joel*

I've met just about every big producer in the world once and had dinner with them, and never once came away impressed. A lot of them are incredible shits. You wouldn't believe it. Real shits. You don't even wanna be in the same room with 'em. They just sit there and scream at you, especially the English ones. Like, "Fuck you! How'd you ever get a fucking record deal?" They think they're psyching you up to play a guitar solo and you just wanna go kill 'em.

*Tom Verlaine, Television*

Learn how to play two chords and then get yourself an attorney before learning the third.

*Tony Iommi, Black Sabbath*

Rock and Roll is a lot like poker. All you need is one good hand.

*Alan Mann, Philadelphia rocker*

Well, they always say that the entertainment and restaurant industries are the only businesses that don't sink during a depression or a recession. I've done both, and I recommend to anyone who wants to be a rock star, if that doesn't pan out, become a cook.

*Chris Cornell, Soundgarden*

You're a local band until you get a record contract and then all of a sudden Bruce Springsteen is your competition.

*Sammy (Llanas) BoDean, the BoDeans*

The people that we want to reach watch Dick Clark. And we found that we've done Dick Clark now about six times. Dick Clark has been without a doubt the most courteous, most cooperative, and least censorship-minded outfit that we've ever done anything for on the tube.

*John Kay, Steppenwolf*

I remember sitting in the back seat of a limousine in 1965, and I was the unhappiest person in the world. My driver said, "What's wrong with you, man? How can you be depressed?" And I replied, "Because I may never be on top again. There's no way this can last."

*Del Shannon*

Pop music is just long hours, hard work and lots of drugs.
*Cass Elliot, the Mamas and the Papas,*
*joking to a reporter*

People think I'm a rich musician. Let me describe my position. Way down.

*Alex Chilton*

I don't make culture—I just sell it. I'm the storekeeper. The shelves are empty. I put the stock on. I make no comment pro or con.

*Dick Clark*

People think you're always having a great time, with Rolls-Royces, money and so on. If they knew the truth, they'd be disillusioned. It's a lot more hard work than fun . . . a lot more fun than working in a jam factory in Hereford.

*Martin Chambers, the Pretenders*

But artists are still artists and record companies will always find new ways to exploit them. And right now, this is a deliberate attempt on my part to be exploited, once again.

*Mitch Ryder*

We don't want to censor your songs. What we want to do is change your song. You're the younger generation; you believe in change.

*Paul Kantner, Jefferson Airplane/Starship, quoting*
*Rocco Laginestra, president of RCA Records*

Q: What are you going to invest your money in?
A: Money.

*Ringo Starr*

On Monday and Wednesday nights we don't have no cover. We'll give bands $25 to copy posters and a case of beer but they don't get paid.

*Carson Spenser, Toronto club owner,*
*on booking bands*

And another thing you can't mess with is radio. That's another taboo. Don't say anything bad about radio. Radio's the greatest thing that ever happened. And if you say anything different from that, don't expect to be played on it.

*Daryl Hall*

Sound is without color and if sound sells it is broadcast on radio via recordings. But national TV in the U.S. has yet to grasp the point that Otis Redding sells more records than Frank Sinatra and Dean Martin and therefore his audience is greater.

*Ralph J. Gleason, critic, 1967*

We were interested in the business of being in rock 'n' roll and being a pop group. Successful, money, cars, that sort of thing. Good living. I mean that's the reason most people get involved in rock music, because they want that sort of success. If you don't, you get involved in something else.

*Nick Mason, Pink Floyd*

They sign up every damn idiot who can string two chords together. The sooner they start telling these gits, "I'm sorry, but you're crap. Go back and learn how to play," the better things will get.

*Nick Lowe*

You know, Mozart and Beethoven never got royalty checks.

*Joe Walsh, on his commercial success in his lifetime*

Q: What made you decide to record "Hippy Hippy Shake?"
A: We just wanted to record something that everybody would want to buy.

*Norman Kuhkle, the Swinging Blue Jeans*

I wasn't at all surprised Ziggy Stardust made my career. I packaged a totally credible plastic rock star—much better than any sort of Monkees fabrication. My plastic rocker was much more plastic than anybody's.

*David Bowie*

If you're gonna sell out, make sure they're buying.

*Martha Davis, the Motels*

This is glamorous, yeah: You drag your butt all over the world. It's a regular job.

*Rick Neilsen, Cheap Trick*

I don't intend to wind up parking cars somewhere.

*Keith Moon*

Our managers found us at the Whiskey A Go Go and then hyped us and stole all our money! I lost $60,000 to them. . . . They legally stole it. . . . I'm one of the most bitter people I know when it comes to the Hollywood music scene.

*Neil Young*

Somebody said to me, "But the Beatles were antimaterialistic." That's a huge myth. John and I literally used to sit down and say, "Now, let's write a swimming pool."

*Paul McCartney*


I don't know anything about music. In my line I don't have to.

*Elvis Presley, 1957*


When you start out, you make one or two records that put you solidly in debt with the record company. Then, if your third record makes some money, you have to pay back at the record company, and if you're lucky, you have enough money to live for a year. Then, after that, the band is bigger, you have to expand your organization and do more professional shows, so you're sort of back in debt again. You never really catch up; for those first five years you're probably better off on the dole.

*Adam Clayton, U2*


I have it figured. See, I'll never ever play for less than $1,000 a night. So someday I'll get a call from some twenty-two-year-old punk promoter and he'll say he really wants me but he can only offer $950. And I'll tell him, "Congratulations son, you've just become the man who retired the great Chuck Berry."

*Chuck Berry*

But once I'm done with something, except to protect people who love the songs, I don't care if they chop it up and package it any way they want. And I don't think that pop music is that much more exalted than the making of commercials.

*Randy Newman*

We're a product and we appeal to a certain type of person. But we try not to let that bother us at all. We just really try to concentrate on making a good record.

*Andrew Fletcher, Depeche Mode*

We're all terminal in this business. When it's over it's over. Unless you want to spend the rest of your life working honky tonks for low pay, see that your pension is taken care of.

*Hal Blaine, legendary session drummer*

Bill Graham was the star of the '60s. He's done more for rock 'n' roll than anyone. More than any of the performers. Because he put on their stages for them. And he opened doors. In the beginning there was great talent, but there were no sound systems. No microphones. Graham came along and changed it. He made the performers a stage. He was what Alan Freed was to the '50s.

*Marty Balin, Jefferson Airplane/Starship*

These guys are like hawkers on the street at a peep show. They promise people the many glorious things that are inside the door, but when you go in, you find out it's $15 for a beer.
*Steve Albini, producer, on the major record companies*

Sometimes we lose our temper with people like record company executives or whatever. I often feel like slapping them around the face.

*Brian Johnson, AC/DC*

Rock & roll is mutating into something else at the moment. . . . Images are everything, and we want to be there when the sort of audiovisual-microchip-interactive music is born.

*Bono*

Didn't Dave Clark say that success in pop music is like being let into a bank vault with a shovel and you don't know how long you've got so you shovel like mad?

*Ed Bicknell, manager of Dire Straits*

I think that record companies should hire psychologists, instead of record promo people, to keep their bands unified and thinking of music in a completely right-side-of-the-brain way—just concentrating on music, not worrying about anything else. All the money stuff will take care of itself. Money is a byproduct of good music.

*Stone Gossard, Pearl Jam*

I opened the door for a lot of people, and they just ran through and left me holding the knob.

*Bo Diddley*

Once you start to care about anything or anybody, it always fucks ambition up.

*Marianne Faithfull*

I'm trying to get the other guys in the band to realize that we're in a business and that it has nothing to do with whether we like each other as human beings.

*Felix Cavaliere, the (reunited) Rascals*

The Man can't bust our music.

*from a Columbia Records ad in the late 1960s*

I'm an observer and a presenter.

*Dick Clark*

The first person I put on that morning was a kid who had been living in a parking lot for ten days. I said to the audience, "Someday, this might happen to you. You know, we all have dreams." He sang one song and he's been writing me ever since.

*Bill Graham, on Live Aid*

I just think it's a really weird job. I'm not saying it's a bad job, I'm not saying it's a great job. But you know, it's just the work that goes into being that athletic. I mean, do you want to go out every night and jump off, like, your car? And have to do that? It becomes your job.

*Axl Rose, Guns N' Roses*

If rock can change the business world, what can't it do? . . . This society works on money. Change the way the money-changers change money and you change the society. Rock is doing that.

*Ralph J. Gleason, critic, 1968*

Paul McCartney at one time was very concerned about our career and he wrote us a letter saying that we had to drop the Byrd glasses and the twelve-string. No alternatives suggested. Merely just get rid of them. A very cryptic note actually.

*Roger McGuinn, the Byrds*

We paid our sound guy more than we paid ourselves. So many guys that coulda been great . . . instead of that new truck they really need, they'll put a pool in their backyard, right at a crucial time.

*Rick Neilsen, Cheap Trick, on how the band reinvested its money in equipment*

The music business has never been a sanctuary of saints. It's been the garment industry rejects. And it's the orphan of the entertainment industry in terms of people who don't make it in the movie industry: They go into the music business.

*Billy Joel*

The pop music chart is a battlefield. It kills me, it kills them, it kills him. It's a war.

*Bob Cowsill, the Cowsills*

All of those business people should be fucking frightened. They don't think that I am anything much. I am not stupid and they should be scared of me. And worried.

*Billy Idol*

The commerciality which rock 'n' roll wallows in has so affected the systems of meaning and meaningfulness that rock 'n' roll may be bringing about the end of the world. . . .

*R. Meltzer, critic*

# long live rock!

There'll always be some arrogant little brat who wants to make noise with a guitar. Rock & roll will never die.

*Dave Edmunds*

I invented rock 'n' roll. Jimi Hendrix was my guitar player. James Brown was my vocalist.

*Little Richard*

It will be gone by June.

Variety, *1955, on rock and roll*

Rock & Roll is a communicable disease.

New York Times, *1956*

Rock & Roll is trying to convince girls to pay money to be near you.

*Richard Hell*

I think Rock and Roll has unlimited potential to talk about anything it wants to, that's my opinion. It can do something movies and plays can't do because it's so short. They're different. It's apples and oranges. You can't compare them. Each has its strength. All three are something great to do.

*Lou Reed*

**17**

All the shit they play on the radio today—it lacks the true meaning of rock, which is sex, subversion, and style. Rock 'n' roll is pagan and primitive and very jungle, and that's how it should be. The moment it stops being those things, it's dead.

*Malcolm McLaren*

Rock can be seen as one attempt to break out of this dead and soulless universe and reassert the universe of magic.

*William S. Burroughs, writer, 1975*

True rock 'n' roll has no form, it's nebulous. . . . The main purpose of rock 'n' roll is celebration of the self. And the only evil in rock 'n' roll is deliberately directed mindlessness— which is a good definition for evil in general.

*Daryl Hall*

See, rock-and-roll, as a form of music on paper, is very simple. But there are variations you can get in there, and one of the biggest ones is with time, and with phrasing. A lot of it's instinct. Once you spot something, you just grab a hold of it and say, "O.K., let's see where it goes." Really, there's no grand strategy. There's no great brain behind this thing. Ha!

*Keith Richards*

Is it just about cucumbers down the trousers? Or is it about genuine people trying to say something?

*Billy Bragg, on the music industry*

We like rock & roll subjects: money, power, sex, death, motorbikes.
I feel what we do is rock & roll 1993.
Our ambition is to be the last band ever.

*members of Sheep on Drugs*

That's why I got into the rock 'n' roll business to begin with: to get out. It made me feel stuff, it made me feel good. I remember the day: I was a senior in high school. It was a beautiful spring day, and I was looking out the window and I realized: If I become a lawyer, I'm going to be sitting just like this, uncomfortable, with weird grease forming on my face, and my neck all red and tight, with people I hate. But if I was a musician, I'd be out there right now. I'd be doing what I wanted. I'd be free.

*Iggy Pop*

Rock and roll is simply an attitude. You don't have to play the greatest guitar.

*Johnny Thunders*

I describe rock-and-roll life as living on a Japanese bullet train. Most of the time what happens is you get rock performers who have a hit album or singles or whatever and then you get people saying, "You gotta keep doing it; you gotta make another record right now, you gotta do this, you gotta do that." You get burned out really quickly and you also don't keep the artistic punch you had doing your best work.

If you stay on that train and don't get off, you tend to lose sight of what got you on the train to start with.

*Meatloaf*

The ideology of rock—the arguments about what records mean, what rock is for—has always been articulated more clearly by fans than by musicians (or businessmen).

*Simon Frith, critic*

Some people paint Picassos and some people fingerpaint. Rock & Roll is a unique combination. Combination. Not one or the other.

*David Lee Roth*

Rock 'n' roll is a term that's been heavily abused. It's not something you can buy in a record shop. It's an attitude.

*Adam Clayton, U2*

There is a lot of kindness and compassion in Rock & Roll. That may sound strange, but it's true.

*Kim Fowley, promoter/manager*

I know that rock 'n' roll changed my life. It was something for me to hold on to. I had nothing. Before then the whole thing was a washout for me. It really gave me a sense of myself, and it allowed me to become useful, which I think most people want to be.

*Bruce Springsteen*

Rock & Roll is a kind of musical newspaper for people who don't like to read.

*Marc Storace, Krokus*

Probably the best work the English have done since the empire. We took it and ran with it. . . .

*Keith Richards*

After like 1950 somehow I tuned out. I have no appreciation whatsoever, zero, for stuff that came after that. I don't know how to explain it. I mean, the thing of Elvis escapes me 100 percent. I don't want to knock the guy, but to me it just didn't mean anything. And nothing that came after it meant anything, either. So much of it sounded like just eardrum-busting noise—and the incredibly self-conscious lyrics, message lyrics, whether they were social or psychological.

*Woody Allen*

Listen to the rock 'n' roll of the '50s. They weren't doing a million notes a second, but those are the records that are carved in stone. If an alien came down and asked me what rock 'n' roll is I'd play them "Hound Dog" or something by Chuck Berry.

*Jeff Beck*

Rock and roll is a means of pulling the white man down to the level of the Negro. It is part of a plot to undermine the morals of the youth of our nation.

*secretary of the North Alabama*
*White Citizens Council, 1956*

You know, there's this place where a river runs into an ocean and the fresh water and the salt water all get mixed in together. And that's what America is all about, and that's what American music is about and that's what rock & roll is about. It actually wasn't invented by anybody, and it's not just black and white, either. It's Mexican and Appalachian and Gaelic and everything that's come floating down the river.

*T-Bone Burnette*

The operative word here is shiny. Rock 'n' roll looked shiny and it sounded shiny. It made a tingle throughout my body. I hadn't done any drugs yet, but it was like what drugs would do later, when you take a heavy hit of something and it gets up your spinal cord.

*Iggy Pop*

Rock and roll is a bit like Las Vegas: guys dressed up in their sisters' clothes pretending to be rebellious and angry but not really angry about anything.

*Sting*

Rock and Roll is the folk music of the electronic age.

*Roger McGuinn, the Byrds*

One of the greatest contradictions of rock 'n' roll is that it's very personal, private music made on a huge public address system.

*Bono*

Rock 'n' roll is a very, very important and vital thing. It changed my life and I know it changed a lot of people's lives. For people to say otherwise is just . . . well, they don't know what they're talking about. I know what it's like to really feel down and alone, and man, the music can have the power to make all those things go away. How can people not understand that?

*Nils Lofgren*

Rock 'n' roll was a place to put everything. You could have pictures in your head and make pictures into words, and the music would carry the words along, like a big bloody boat. And that's what everybody started to do.

*John Lennon, 1975*

Rock is so much fun. That's what it's all about — filling up the chest cavities and the empty kneecaps and elbows.

*Jimi Hendrix*

I think that for any generation to assert itself as an aware human entity, it has to break with the past, so obviously the kids that are coming along next are not going to have much in common with what we feel. They're going to create their own unique sound. Things like wars and monetary cycles get involved too. Rock 'n' roll probably could be explained by . . . it was after the Korean War was ended . . . and there was a psychic purge.

*Jim Morrison*

There is a pulse, a flow of rock 'n' roll that has never gone down a notch in the least since Chuck Berry first realized you could take the guitar beyond a rhythm instrument. I'd argue that to the end of the earth.

*Ted Nugent*

I mean, wouldn't you rather listen to a dumb song that makes you rock and roll?

*Dan Baird, ex Georgia Satellites*

Rock 'n' roll is like a drug. I don't take very much rock 'n' roll, but when I do rock 'n' roll, I fuckin' do it. But I don't want to do it all the time 'cause it'll kill me. The way I do it, I don't want to fuck around with it. It's just like a drug. When you're singing and playing rock 'n' roll, you're on the leading edge of yourself. You're tryin' to vibrate, tryin' to make something happen. It's like there's somethin' alive and exposed.

*Neil Young*

We like this kind of music. Jazz is strictly for the stay-at-homes.

*Buddy Holly*

Rock and roll has never completely made its peace with the industry that sponsors it, or with the society that it inhabits, though there have been periods of concession and co-option on both sides.

*Jann S. Wenner, publisher of* Rolling Stone

What is this thing called rock 'n' roll? Some of it's sex, some of it's drugs, some of it's hope, some of it's tragedy, some of it's family, some of it is just driving a car down the freeway and trying to pretend there is a tomorrow when there isn't. Originally it was music that came from people that were in trouble, and spoke deeply and hugely and heroically from deep down in their soul. That's what we inherit here today. It's a real living, breathing religion—that's how I feel about it.

*Pete Townshend, remarks at the ground-breaking*
*ceremony for the Rock and Roll Hall*
*of Fame Museum in Cleveland, 1993*

The trouble with rock 'n' roll is that it's sex, man. Folk music is different. Take the cock out of rock and it's nothing. It's not relevant.

*Don McLean*

Rock & roll is basically blue-collar music. This is a working-class town. There's not much else to do, you know. Bars. But when you go to a bar, what're they playing? Rock & roll music.

*Kid Leo (Lawrence J. Travagliante), disc jockey at WMMS-FM, Cleveland, 1979*

It's not music, it's a disease.

*Mitch Miller*

If your parents don't hate it, it ain't rock 'n' roll.

*Jim Dickinson, producer*

What the purists forget is that "rock & roll" means much more than just the music. Anyone who ever took those words to heart knows that; knows that there are books and movies and people and events and attitudes that matter more to a rock & roll way of life than do many records that are labeled rock & roll. Jack Kerouac was rock & roll; Bobby Rydell was not. Tom Robbins is rock & roll; Andy Gibb is not. Star Wars is rock & roll; A Star Is Born is not.

*Chet Flippo, critic, 1977*

I like rock & roll; I don't like much else.

*John Lennon*

In the end, I realized that rock & roll wasn't just about finding fame and wealth. Instead, for me, it was about finding your place in the world, figuring out where you belong.

*Bruce Springsteen*

The best rock & roll music encapsulates a certain high energy—an angriness—whether on record or onstage. That is, rock & roll is only rock & roll if it's not safe. You know, one of the things I hate is what rock & roll has become in a lot of people's hands: a safe, viable vehicle for pop. . . . It's like, rock & roll—the best kind, that is, the real thing—is always brash. That's the reason for punk. I mean, what was punk about? Violence and energy—and that's really what rock & roll's all about.

*Mick Jagger*

Rock music has become a plague of messages about sexual promiscuity, bisexuality, incest, sado-masochism, satanism, drug use, alcohol abuse and constantly, misogyny. The lyrics regarding these things are celebratory, encouraging or at least desensitizing.

*George Will, political columnist, 1985*

Rock swings with a heavy backbeat and it's done that for twenty-five years. It's supposed to be fun and that's why I like it. It's dance music. But it hasn't really progressed musically. . . . Heavy backbeat, that's what it is.

*Charlie Watts, the Rolling Stones*

If you are a student, a professor, a parent, this is your life because you already know that rock and roll is more than just music; it is the energy center of the new culture and youth revolution.

*from* Rolling Stone *magazine's first ad in*
The New York Times

For the reality of what's happening today in America, we must go to rock 'n' roll, to popular music.

*Ralph J. Gleason, critic, 1967*

In just about every country except England and America there are strangely strong family ties. Very few countries need rock & roll. Very few. It's America and England that need it, and probably Germany. But France and Italy, no way. They don't need it. Rock provides a family life that is missing in America and England. It provides a sense of community.

*David Bowie*

Rock and roll? The true ones are going to stay in it. The fakes and phonies have to fall down by the wayside because the road is too strong for them to walk. But it's your life. Like me, show business is my life. I've dedicated my whole entire life to it. All of it, yeah. Beautiful.

*Little Richard*

I'm amazed at the spirituality in rock & roll. People who criticize it only hear the surface. They don't hear the heart and soul.

*Johnny Cash*

The ideal rock star is young, male, horny and well hung.
*Robert Pattison, critic*

Rock and roll defined youth as puberty and transformed adolescents into a market, an interest group, and a generation.
*Robert Christgau, the Andre Malraux of rock and roll*

The other thing was that we were aware of the high degree of incompatibility between jazz and rock music. And that it didn't take very much jazz to offend a rock listener pretty badly in a way they would never, ever forgive.
*Walter Becker, Steely Dan*

Music today is a bunch of groaning, whining, pseudo-serious, angst-ridden dolts. At some point rock 'n' roll became rock then it became big business, and now it's just some ugly marketing thing. My job—I was put here to stir up some shit—is to be the Cheez Whiz in the caviar of life.
*Mojo Nixon*

My songs do make perfect songs for other bands because they're so easy to play. That's one of the things I like about rock 'n' roll. You can sit down and learn how to play it. It's democracy. It's not jazz.

*Lou Reed*

I think we're being duped. That we're pawns. I think that's why I wanted to be in rock 'n' roll, because I felt that, yeah, if I did just do a normal nine-to-five job I really was stuck. Some people might look at it like it's a frivolous existence, but Christ—at least I don't feel quite so controlled.

*Billy Idol*

I don't think it's rock unless it is in some way extreme. Unless you come off totally fucked-up and go home completely destroyed you don't feel like you've achieved anything.

*Pete Townshend*

I've always liked the intensity of heavy rock. I've noticed that most of it is born out of frustration. The original idea of rock 'n' roll is that it was always meant to be one big fuck-up, just like Sid Vicious. I never really went for that idea.

*Robert Palmer*

Russians cannot rock. Maybe it's a purely Anglo-Saxon talent. We've had maybe three good bands in 20 years. Every time I see a guitar in Russian hands, it looks wrong.

*Andrei Tumanov, Russian critic*

Rock 'n' roll might best be summed up as monotony tinged with hysteria.

*Vance Packard, social critic, testifying before the Senate Subcommittee on Interstate Commerce, 1958*

Commercial rock 'n' roll music is a brutalization of the stream of contemporary Negro church music . . . an obscene looting of a cultural expression.

*Ralph Ellison, writer, 1964*

The martial music of every sideburned delinquent on the face of the earth.

*Frank Sinatra*

I don't know which will go first—rock 'n' roll or Christianity.

*John Lennon, 1966*

# everybody's a critic

The Beatles are not merely awful . . . they are so unbelievably horrible, so appallingly unmusical, so dogmatically insensitive to the magic of the art that they qualify as crowned heads of antimusic.

*William F. Buckley, writer, 1964*

Hell no! Everyone is either bald or dead or looks like a plum pudding.

*Joan Baez, on reunion concerts*

I don't like that "We're going to save you" attitude. One way or another, you're going to hear the U2 album, whether you want to or not. I think they're a heap of crap. If I want to be on earth, I have to deal with Bono. He's the arch villain.

*Henry Rollins*

"Stairway to Heaven" was the most famous rock song in Western civilization in the '70s because it was the best rock song in Western civilization in the '70s. . . . Also proof that words don't have to mean anything to be meaningful. I mean, what's this "If there's a bustle in your hedgerow don't be alarmed now?" If I found anything bustling in my hedgerow I'd get out my shotgun.

*Chuck Eddy, critic*

The lyrics to "Stairway to Heaven" are horrible, nothing more than nonsense words enlivened by cliché. If I ever wrote "There's a lady who's sure all that glitters is gold," my editor would cancel my contract.

*Jimmy Guterman, critic*

It sounds like a cliché, but he's the only one I can think of who really hasn't sold out. His voice sounds the same. He hasn't really changed his sound. He hasn't tried to update it.

*Kim Gordon, Sonic Youth, on Neil Young*

This is an age of glitter and flamboyance. People like Cyndi Lauper realize this. She is smart. She knows the flashier-looking you are the better. Prince is smart.

*Liberace, 1985*

God is Love
Love is blind.
Ray Charles is blind.
Ray Charles is God.

*graffiti that used to reside over the urinal*
*in the Maple Leaf Bar, New Orleans*

As far as rock is concerned, English is the language that mattered. I've played with Spanish bands in Mexico and I can tell you that rock in Spanish just doesn't fit. And blues even worse. You can't imagine how bad a 12-bar phrase sounds in another language. Everybody just has to sing them in English.

*Alfredo "Fito" de la Parra, Canned Heat*

"Jumpin' Jack Flash" is my fucking favorite of all Stones songs.

*Keith Richards*

I can tell you flatly, he can't last.
*Jackie Gleason, on Elvis Presley, 1956*

I'd rather see Liza Minelli than any rock performer.
*Adam Ant*

Michael Jackson, he used to watch me from the wings and got his moon walk from my camel walk—he'll tell you if you ask. Same way I was slippin' and slidin' before Prince was out of his crib; that's why Alan Leeds who used to work for my organization is on his management team, tipping and hipping him. I ain't jealous, I'm zealous! I ain't teased, I'm pleased! Who's gonna do James Brown better'n James Brown? Think!
*James Brown*

I don't know what goes on upstairs with him. To me it's pretty simple. Get an alarm clock, ya know?
*Izzy Stradlin, ex Guns N' Roses, on Axl Rose's chronic lateness in starting shows*

The Grateful Dead, by and large, are a bunch of perverse gunsels.

*Bob Weir, Grateful Dead*

---

# radio, radio

You know the Perry Como show back in the '60s? Where he'd come out and sit on the stool with his cool sweater? That's where rock 'n' roll is today. There are a few exceptions. But generally we've got this crap produced by dicknoses, I mean, people putting out what they know will sell and people saying "play that" to 150 radio stations who can't make up their own minds and are paying these idiots to tell them what to do. It's a wild situation.

*Neil Young*

The radio stands for brainwashing, dictating and telling people what they should be listening to and buying. That's why we're in the state we're in, why rock 'n' roll is in such pathetic state. Hopefully, things are gonna get better, y'know? I mean, we don't live in the past. We live for the betterment of rock 'n' roll.

*Joey Ramone, the Ramones*

A lot of these bands try to be heavy. They can park their car next to heavy, they can get their car to the heavy shopping mall, but they're never going to get heavy. And to me that is where they're at.

*Henry Rollins*

When I hear something that I really love, the hair on my arm stands up and I get goosebumps—and this song does that to me.

*Eddie Van Halen, on Peter Gabriel's "Red Rain"*

The only term I won't accept is "genius." The term "genius" gets used far too loosely in rock & roll.

*Jimmy Page*

What we all fail to understand is that the majority of rock and roll stars are diaper people, relative to how to handle an audience. How long have some of the great money-earners of today been in the business?

*Bill Graham, promoter, Fillmores East and West*

Chuck Berry was the first one to capture the cadence of American speech in song.

*John Sebastian*

Rock stars are horrible people. Being a street cleaner or a baker is a more honorable profession.

*Michael Hutchence, INXS*

This group the Sex Pistols pukes on stage? I don't necessarily like that. That's not showmanship. . . . They gotta get themselves an act.

*Bo Diddley, 1978*

But there are a lot of these English, second-generation whatever-they're-called bands, the substance of which, and the sources from which they draw their influences, are no longer Howlin' Wolf and Robert Johnson—they're me and Steve Marriott. There's a handful of people they listen to and they don't listen to anybody else. . . . They just listen to what's commercially successful, ape it, come over here, sell four million records, sell out four nights at the Spectrum, and bludgeon everybody's ears with something that has no representation of subtlety at all.

*Robert Plant, Led Zeppelin*

The Faces were my favorite band of all time. I think they were the best band ever. Period.

*Paul Westerberg, the Replacements*

She sounded like she worked in Sears.

*Nick Lowe, on why he wanted
to produce Chrissie Hynde*

Rock musicians are America's most wasted natural resource.

*Camille Paglia, writer*

The only mathematical guitar genius I've ever run into who does not offend my intestinal nervousness with his rearguard sound.

*Bob Dylan, on Robbie Robertson*

I know my records will click, so I just make fewer.

*Phil Spector*

I don't like the provinces. You can't eat and you can't get clean shirts.

*Mick Jagger*

Lou Reed is my hero because he stands for all the fucked up things that I could ever possibly conceive of—which probably only shows the limits of my imagination.

*Lester Bangs, critic*

It will replace nothing except suicide.

*Cher, on hearing the Velvet Underground*
*for the first time*

Los Angeles is awful—like Liverpool with palm trees.

*Johnny Rotten*

A cross between Joan Crawford and Marlene Dietrich doing a glitter revival of New Faces!

*Mr. Blackwell, fashion critic, on David Bowie, 1973*

**39**

The amusing thing about this is its supreme unimportance—after it's all over, and they've outsold everyone else in history, the Monkees will still leave absolutely no mark on American music.

> Crawdaddy! *magazine, 1967, as*
> *the group dominated the charts*

I don't think there are too many people who are capable of it. Maybe one. Joni Mitchell. That's the music that I play at home all the time, Joni Mitchell. *Court and Spark* I love because I'd always hoped that she'd work with a band.

> *Jimmy Page, on "consistent, total brilliance"*

Perestroika and glasnost killed Russian rock. When the K.G.B. forced rock underground, the music wasn't great but its social and spiritual and political significance was tremendous. Now, the bands are stupid and unimaginative. They have no idea what to sing about or how to do it. Russia may be a great nation but, in rock-and-roll terms, it has no more influence than does Finland.

> *Artemy Troitsky, Russian critic*

The audience in London is very similar to the audience in L.A.—which is to say, singularly boring and jaded.

> *Frank Zappa, 1978*

Today's groups differ from the Andrews Sisters and the Ames Brothers in that their music is more direct and emotional. It is also more mystical and very often "way out." I think that this is an age of experimentation. Some of the present forms may not last long. Only time will tell.

*Ed Sullivan, 1970*

There were two types of Rock & Roll that had become bankrupt to me. One was "Look at me, I've got a hairy chest and a big willy!" and the other was the "Fuck me, I'm sensitive" Jackson Browne school of seduction. They're offensive and mawkish and neither has any real pride or confidence.

*Elvis Costello*

# i write the songs

But art is the last thing I'm worried about when I write a song. I don't think it really matters. If you want to call it art, yeah, okay, you can call it what you like. As far as I'm concerned, "Art" is just short for "Arthur."

*Keith Richards*

I think that each record reflects the mood of the year that you wrote the songs and did the record. I can look back at some of the older Stones records and think, "That wasn't really a very good record. But that was that year. That's what we did."

*Mick Jagger*

Well, I don't write them unless I absolutely have to. I don't wake up in the morning and say: "Jeez, I feel great today. I think I'll write a song." I mean, anything is more interesting to me than writing a song. It's like "I think I'd like to write a song. . . . No, I guess I better go feed the cat first." You know what I mean? It's like pulling teeth. I don't enjoy it a bit.

*Jerry Garcia*

I'm a musician by default. It's just that I can express my emotions better in songs.

*Pete Shelley, the Buzzcocks*

If you just wrote about what you know, we wouldn't have had 90 percent of the art in the world.

*Peter Buck, R.E.M.*

I don't think I've written any melodies as good as most TV show themes in the '50s.

*Tom Verlaine, Television*

Everybody feels like they want to put a notch in life, no matter who you are. That's what my songs are. It's like a guy who swings a hammer or a sculptor or someone who lays linoleum. It's what I can contribute.

*Louie Perez, Los Lobos*

Rock 'n' roll has a potential for evil—far beyond any conception of it as "the Devil's music"—simply because it runs away, it belies any sort of responsibility. If you write from that perspective, you don't have any morality or responsibility.

*Elvis Costello*

Hell, we steal. We're the robber barons of rock 'n' roll.

*Donald Fagen, Steely Dan*

When I'm writing songs the minutes are like hours. I sit there with nothing — just a big picture of [rock critic] Greil Marcus in my head hanging over the piano.

*Randy Newman*

It's almost like a survival instinct — it's that primitive. If I ignore my work, I start having anxiety attacks, I can't really sleep well, my eating habits become erratic, I get irritable. It starts taking its toll in a very physical and mental way. It's almost like the energy is there, and if I don't use it as it was intended, it turns toxic.

*Roseanne Cash, on her creativity*

I didn't remember saying this, but somebody quoted me saying at a show that I write about cities the way some people write about lovers. Joni Mitchell's always in and out of love affairs; well, I was always in and out of cities.

*Michelle Shocked*

To me, my creation is not from a logical thought pattern. It's from a sub-dominant hemisphere of the brain. When I'm really writing, really playing, I'm not thinking at all. I'm just there, feeling it — and in it. That's what I want; I'll do anything to get that.

*Neil Young*

The best songs come from being depressed, or just bored of everything you're supposed to do.

*Paul Westerberg, the Replacements*

I've been thinking about this recently. I find that when I write a really good song, it's a blur in my mind when I actually wrote it. I know the song exists, 'cause I can play it for my friends, but I just can't remember what happened between thinking of the idea of the song and finally playing it for my friends. Something happened that I don't remember.

*Joe Strummer, the Clash*

But if there's not sickness in a song, it's not worth singing.

*Iggy Pop*

Definitely, songwriting is the greatest satisfaction in the world, the ultimate high. Nothing beats writing a song and thinking it's the best one in the world. Y'know, calling up the rest of the guys and telling them I just wrote the greatest song in the world and they have to learn it right away. Know what I mean?

*Joey Ramone, the Ramones*

All my favorite records are short; the kind that when they're over you wish they weren't.

*Marshall Crenshaw*

The mid-'70s was the age of the singer-songwriter, which for my money really screwed things up.

*John Hiatt, singer/songwriter*

If I could have thought of something better, I would have, but that's all I could come up with that day. Sometimes you find when you say something too directly, it lets you down.

*Robbie Robertson, on songwriting*

That's the thing about rock 'n' roll. People understand writing about personal relationships, cars and food; but once you start to tread heavier water they question it.

*Mick Jagger*

Once the songs have been recorded and put on vinyl they are someone else's entertainment and not ours.

*Robert Smith, the Cure*

What I like to do is put myself in the first person. People can listen when you have a problem. But they don't like it when you tell them that they have a problem.

*MC Lyte*

You know how I learned to write songs? I went to a poetry class for one day, and then dropped out. The one thing I learned that day was a poem must have three things. It must have the visual, the sensual, and the emotional. Want to hear an example? "Sunshine on my shoulder makes me happy . . . "

*Ethan Buckler, King Kong*


Many of my songs I dreamed fully realized. I dream I am in the control room, listening to something on the speakers, and it is this piece of music that I have not written yet. . . . This has happened so frequently that I can wake myself up and remember substantial parts.

*Todd Rundgren*


I write songs no matter what mood I'm in; it's my work, dig?

*Smokey Robinson*


I do my best work when I'm in pain and turmoil.

*Sting*


I guess it was a good title, because I heard it on classic rock radio twice today.

*Chris Frantz, Talking Heads, on*
*"Burning Down the House"*


I don't want to sell my music. I'd like to give it away because where I got it, you didn't have to pay for it.

*Captain Beefheart*


When I walk the dog, I get ideas.

*Andy Partridge, XTC*

Many of them think writing lyrics to pop songs is easy: You write about boys and girls falling in and out of love, and that's it. I tell them that I go to the library to research my songs; that I write and rewrite; that the greatest satisfaction is knowing I worked really hard and tried to do the best I could . . .

*Natalie Merchant, 10,000 Maniacs, on students*
*participating in a national songwriting contest*

You can get in a taxi and just have him drive and start writing down words you see, information that is in your normal view: dry cleaners, custom tailors, alterations, electrical installations, Dunlop safety center, lease, broker, sale . . . just start making a list of words that you see. And then you just kind of give yourself an assignment. You say, "I'm going to write a song and I'm going to use all these words in that song."

*Tom Waits*

But let's remember the essence of popular music. A song comes on. What do you hear first? Words? Nah, you hear a beat, then a melody. Take "My Sharona." If you really liked the song, then you took the time to dig out the words, and they're pubescent, dumbo words, but they fit the song.

*Billy Joel*

You make records for other people, not for yourself. That's what it's about. I'm making it for the marketplace. After I write it, I don't think about it. I just go on to the next part of life.

*Van Morrison*

All through this I've always felt that if you thought of it all as a book, then you have the Great American Novel, every record as a chapter. They're all in chronological order. You take the whole thing, stack it and listen to it in order, there's my Great American Novel.

*Lou Reed*

In a popular song you've only got three minutes and two-and-a-half verses—you have to get to the point.

*Richard Thompson*

Fourteen- and 15-year-olds are really intense. They write in journals and they think really deep thoughts and they spend a lot of time being real philosophers in a way I think we lose as we get older and worry about earning a living.

*Janis Ian*

"Eight Miles High." We got the idea from listening to John Coltrane in our mobile home.

*Roger McGuinn, the Byrds*

When I wrote the first five or six hit songs for the Who, I was completely and totally alone. I had no girlfriend, no friends,

no nothing—it was me addressing the world. That's where
the power of that early stuff comes from.

*Pete Townshend*

Songs. Songs. People think you're a songwriter. They think
you wrote it, that it's all yours, that you're totally responsible
for it. Really, you are just a medium, you know. You just de-
velop a facility for recognizing and picking up things and you
just have to be ready to be there, like being at a seance. Whole
songs just come to you, you don't write them. Songs come to
me en masse, virtually out of the air. It's more of being a
medium of the thing coming through you than of you actually creating it. I always get the feeling that it has been on its
way, anyway. "Satisfaction": I just happened to be awake
and to have a guitar in my hand when it arrived.

*Keith Richards*

Like I have, well, a little notebook full of titles, full of one-
lines that can either be a title or part of a song, that sort of
thing. In fact the first page, you know, I really had a streak,
and the first page had . . . "Proud Mary" was the first
thing on it, and somewhere in the middle was "Lodi," "Bad
Moon Rising," and near the end was something called
"Riverboat" and "Rolling on the River." Originally there
were three separate things. Eventually they got together and
became "Proud Mary." I didn't conceive of "Proud Mary" as

a boat at all. I was thinking of a washerwoman or something, you know. It's completely different.

*John Fogerty*

I don't say I ever write for popularity. I check a song by its lyrics. A song ain't nuthin' in the world but a story just wrote with music to it.

*Hank Williams*

It just happens when it happens. Usually, though, I write a song because I need one. I tell myself I need a song. Then I write it. I kind of commission myself to write songs, you know.

*John Fogerty*

Words to me are just the sound of the voice. And the words don't have all the meaning to 'em, 'cause somebody could say the same thing a different bunch of ways and meanings. Words don't really explain it all.

*Dr. John the Night Tripper (Mac Rebennack)*

Generally, the ones that come fast are the best.

*Paul Westerberg, the Replacements*

My big private goal, my actual composing ideal, is to write a thirty-second piece that just totally evokes something.

Everyone will say, "I know just what he means." That's my sort of private thing.

*Ian Anderson, Jethro Tull*

I feel like I'm a goalie. If you lose the game, it's your fault. If you win the game, it was just your job. The goaltender of rock & roll.

*Dave Pirner, on being the songwriter for Soul Asylum*

I want to make my best work then die. I'm not going to stick around long enough to churn out a load of mediocre crap like all those guys from the Sixties. I'd rather kill myself. I have no intention of waiting around to witness my artistic decline.

*Elvis Costello*

You can't hold a note if it's a consonant, so if you're going to have this long note in the melody, it has to be a vowel. You have to be that specific.

*Jerry Garcia, on songwriting with*
*Grateful Dead lyricist Robert Hunter*

I'm not on any crusade or pilgrimage. By and large, what I write is a figment of my imagination and it has to be fairy-tale-like.

*Greg Lake, Emerson, Lake and Palmer*

# i've been six days
# on the road

There was no violence, no one got hurt, but three thousand seats died. It's hard to understand why someone goes, "Gee, I love this band, I'm going to kill my seat." I don't quite understand the connection.

*Lars Ulrich, Metallica*

I love my kids but, Jesus, sometimes I can't wait to get on that tour bus and get the hell out of town.

*Martha Davis, the Motels*

The tour was just, like, a necklace of days spent in flourescently lit rooms . . .

*Evan Dando, the Lemonheads*

What I really remember about the last 10 years, and I hate to say this in a way, is sitting backstage in some dump looking at the ceiling, at those shitty acoustic tiles with the litttle holes in them, thinking, "God, someone's making a million a year with these ugly tiles that every band in the world is going to poke out." It really has been a room, a car, a car, a room, a room, a stage and a car.

*Peter Buck, R.E.M., 1991*

This is the coolest part of the show. Sometimes, when there's been a really crazy show, you can find watches and jewelry and all kinds of stuff on the floor afterward.

> *Dave Grohl, Nirvana, inspecting*
> *a venue's floor after a show*

What you can never get in your book is the utter, total boredom of being in a band [on tour].

> *John Lydon, to writer Jon Savage*

Rock 'n' roll in stadiums is genuinely awful. These concerts are just like Tupperware parties — held in honor of the Great God Tupper — with 50,000 people, only they don't buy Tupperware, they buy hot dogs and T-shirts and occasionally look up to watch those disgusting video screens that are all out of sync and make you feel sick and torture you.

> *Roger Waters*

It's always amazed me that people would want to go to a football stadium to see rock 'n' roll played. I love the tribal shit, but the puritan musician in me is always griping. Musicians are great gripers. Ideally, I know that this stuff sounds best in a room with 2,000 or 3,000 people at the most, when the place is stuffed with bodies and the sound is jamming off them.

> *Keith Richards*

The only thing I could see doing is the opposite of touring, where I stay in one place and the audience tours to see me.

*Brian Eno*

In 1965, we sat down one evening in a hotel and worked out that since the band had started two years earlier, I'd had 278 girls; Brian, 130; Mick, about 30; Keith, six; and Charlie, none.

*Bill Wyman, the Rolling Stones*

I remember going to see John Lennon after that [the Stones' 1969 American tour] and explaining to him what it was like. The Beatles always said, "Well, we don't tour because we can't hear ourselves." I said, "It's not like that anymore. You can go out there and play—people will listen and applaud at the end." But for them, it was already too late.

*Mick Jagger*

Q: What kind of car was it that you drove into a swimming pool?
A: Lincoln.
Q: What kind of pool was it?
A: A standard Holiday Inn swimming pool. The Lincoln was the best thing about it. Then I threw the keys to the valet and told him to park it.

*Keith Moon*

You've been standing around an airport, had some accommodation problem because someone's hair's too long, or you've been in some vehicle for hours without sleep and have only three hours till you go on stage. People in the group start getting uptight, and music's an emotional thing too, you know, so everybody's backstage yelling and screaming. . . . People get really strange getting on and off buses and talking to a lot of different people all the time.

*Grace Slick*

That's why after 1977 I refused to play stadiums, because the larger the audience, the whole thing becomes more about commerce and less about communication, music, human feelings and values.

*Roger Waters*

I have a new house I haven't seen yet, a new car I haven't seen yet and I miss eating food that my wife has cooked for me.

*Kirk Hammett, Metallica*

Readers think the road's great—you get rich, you have a big time. Fact of the business is, you get old on the road, you get tired, you get disgusted, you die.

*Ry Cooder*

The sheriff took me out in the law car, and he puts me on the plane and says [American accent], "Son, don't ever dock in

Flint, Michigan, again." I said, "Dear boy, I wouldn't dream
of it."

*Keith Moon, recalling the aftermath of his twenty-first
birthday party in Flint, during which he orchestrated a
hotel-room food fight and then drove a Lincoln
Continental into the hotel pool*

There are no sick days when you're on tour.

*Billy Joel*

I get bored, you see. There was a time in Saskatoon, in Cana-
da. It was another 'Oliday Inn, and I was bored. Now, when
I get bored, I rebel. I said, "FUCK IT, FUCK THE LOT OF
YA!" And I took out me 'atchet and chopped the 'otel room
to bits. The television. The chairs. The dresser. The cup-
board doors. The bed. The lot of it. Ah-ha-ha-HAHAHA-
HAHAHAHAHAHAHAHA! It happens all the time.

*Keith Moon*

When you play music in a hall designed for basketball, you
take your chances.

*Frank Zappa*

We used to play a game with the Mats on the bus, and it
would be really quiet, and all the sudden you'd point at someone and yell, "Month, day, city, year!" and people would be

like "February, Philadelphia, '92." And it was like March 3rd, '91. And it was serious.

*Paul Westerberg, the Replacements*


Maybe it's more of a pain to find space in the overhead rack, but if you want to see that guitar again, do not check it. It can easily be lost or stolen. Don't even leave it in the rack when the bus is taken out of sight for "cleaning."

*Jonathan Richman*


What some band should do is buy a town and only play *there,* make it a sort of shrine to themselves. That's a good little gag right there. You'd have to be in a band big enough, to pull the people and become a phenomenon. Or you could have several bands, like an ongoing festival. Vegas is the closest thing so far.

*Black Francis, the Pixies*


If you're wondering if we've destroyed a Holiday Inn, well, sometimes it happens. One time, Gregg and I went out and bought 25 extension cords. We figured that the extension cords were just long enough to reach from our room to the first floor. And we took a color television, we plugged it in and tossed it into the pool. It was a wonderful sight. You ever done that? I'm telling you, man, it goes up in beautiful color. It explodes. It's great!

*Steve Perry, Journey*

It's a cool exercise to discover that you can live without a lot of things. When you are on the road four months at a time, possessions are definitely poverty.

*Chris Baron, the Spin Doctors*

# name that band

We started getting letters from some New Jersey bar band who claimed "We've been the Bangs for fourteen years and we do Lynyrd Skynyrd covers and we hear that Miles Copeland is your manager and we want two billion dollars." So we changed our name.

*Vickie Peterson, the Bangles*

Can you imagine? — "Hey, hey — we're the Parrots?" No way.

*Davy Jones, on an early name suggested for the Monkees*

Well, there was this guy who sold tomatoes, this black gentleman, and his name was the Captain. He had beefsteak tomatoes, actually, but he used to say his tomatoes were as big as beef hearts.

*Captain Beefheart, on the origin of his name*

I don't know. We chose the name on Mother's Day.

*Frank Zappa, on the naming of the Mothers of Invention*

El Rayo-X was a boxer from Mexico, and he used to come up and beat the shit out of everybody and then go back to Mexico. I liked it because it sounded very strange.

*David Lindley, El Rayo-X, on his band's name*

The name meant for me all sorts of things. It came about by the idea of a pistol, a pinup, a young thing, a better-looking assassin, a Sex Pistol.

*Malcolm McLaren, manager of the Sex Pistols*

Many people ask what are Beatles? Why Beatles? Ugh, Beatles? How did the name arrive? So we will tell you. It came in a vision—a man appeared on a flaming pie and said unto them, "From this day on you are Beatles with an 'A'." Thank you, Mister Man, they said, thanking him. And so they were Beatles.

*John Lennon, 1960*

A band's name is always one of the critical things to me. If you pick a stupid name, it indicates that you haven't thought too much about the whole thing, and it's a clear indication of where you hold yourself and what you're doing in your own mind. If you give your band a stupid, trivial name, then it indicates that you consider what you do stupid and trivial.

*Dave Thomas, Pere Ubu, whose band is named
after the hero of* Ubu Roi, *a play by Alfred Jarry,
a French absurdist*

Back in the late days of the Acid Tests, we were looking for a name. We'd abandoned the Warlocks, it didn't fit any more. One day we were all over at Phil's house smoking DMT. He had a big Oxford dictionary, opened it, and there was "grateful dead," those words juxtaposed. It was one of those moments, y'know, like everything else on the page went blank, diffuse, just sorta oozed away, and there was GRATEFUL DEAD, big black lettered edged all around in gold, man, blasting out at me, such a stunning combination. So I said, "How about Grateful Dead?" and that was it.

*Jerry Garcia*

Great-grandma Pearl used to make this hallucinogenic preserve that there's total stories about. We don't have the recipe, though.

*Eddie Vedder, Pearl Jam*

I went to a studio in a grey pullover and horrible tweed trousers, and the next day I went in an orange tie, and a bloke told me, "Now you really look like a Kink." Maybe it was an unfortunate name—the sadistic image or the things in your arm. It's a good name, in a way, because it's something people don't really want.

*Ray Davies, the Kinks*

A Mekon was a tyrannical space alien that terrorized earth in a 1950s English comic called "Dan Dare."

*John Langford, the Mekons*

**65**

The name Quicksilver came about because we're all the same astrological sign: Virgo. Gary and Greg are born on the same day. David and I are born on the same day. The four of us were doing our thing. There was a fifth member then, Jimmy Murray, who is a Gemini. Virgos are mercury and mercury is quicksilver and Mercury is a messenger and Virgo is a servant, so Quicksilver Messenger Service.

*John Cipollina, Quicksilver Messenger Service*

The name King Crimson is a synonym for Beelzebub, which is an anglicized form of the Arabic phrase B'il Sabab. This means "the man with an aim" and is the recognizable quality of King Crimson.

*Robert Fripp*

Led Zeppelin is a good name, isn't it? I made it up. Everybody says Keith Moon made it up, but he didn't. About four years ago I was really gettin' fed up with The Who. . . . And I was talking with a fellow who is the production manager for the Led Zeppelin now. I was talking to him down in a club in New York. And I said, "Yeah, I'm thinking of leaving the group and forming my own group. I'm going to call the group Led Zeppelin. And I'm going to have an LP cover with like the Hindenburg going down in flames, and, you know, this whole business." And like two months later he was working for Jimmy Page and, like, they were looking for a name, and so he suggested Led Zeppelin, and Page liked it, and they came out with the same LP cover that I'd planned.

*John Entwistle, the Who*

I've got the perfect name to call you guys: you are now going to be known as "Redwood."

*Brian Wilson, after co-producing an early vocal session of a group that would later become Three Dog Night*

I have no idea. I really don't. It was one day, just boom. We needed a new name and I said, "Why don't we call ourselves . . . " and I could have said Mary Smith, but I said Alice Cooper. And that was the name.

*Alice Cooper (Vincent Damon Furnier)*

A lemonhead is a midwestern candy—yellow spheres that are sweet on the outside and really sour on the inside.

*Evan Dando, the Lemonheads*

I lugged my drums over to this old house on Fountain Avenue. They were paving the streets, I remember. And there was this steamroller out front with a big sign on the side that read Buffalo Springfield. When I walked into the house, the guys were already talking about taking that as a group name, and I thought, "Yeah, what a great name—Buffalo Springfield."

*Dewey Martin, Buffalo Springfield*

We are fascinated by the icons that were around when we were growing up. We're also fascinated by imperfection, and Sandy's imperfection made her beautiful to us.

*Roberto Haraldson, Sandy Duncan's Eye*

We started out with the Crackers. We tried to call ourselves the Honkies. Everybody kind of backed off from that. It was too . . . straight. So we decided just to call ourselves . . . the Band.

*Richard Manuel, the Band*

I went down to the tee-shirt shop and had a shirt printed with "Talking Heads" on it. This guy came up to me in the street and said, "Is that the name of a band? Ohh I hate that!" I knew it had to stay, ha ha ha.

*Chris Frantz, Talking Heads*

# fame! what's your name?

I'm much less of an asshole now than I was when nobody liked us. So at least I know that if I become really famous, nobody will be able to say being famous turned me into a dick.

*J Mascis, Dinosaur Jr*

Success is like having a one-night stand with Lady Di.

*John Waite*

I mean, I never really thought about that before, but those ads everywhere with me half-dressed, showing off in my underwear and posing like I'm grabbing myself, maybe that has something to do with it. It's like people think I'm a smart-ass, not a nice person. They've decided I'm hard, and they're not going to take the time to know me.

*Marky Mark Wahlberg*

My drive in life is from this horrible fear of being mediocre.

*Madonna*

It's irritating when you go into a store and somebody puts on your record. I feel like I should be lip-synching.

*Thurston Moore, Sonic Youth*

In rock 'n' roll, you're built up to be torn down. Like architecture in America, you build it up and let it stand for ten years, then call it shabby and rip it down and put up something else.

*Joni Mitchell*

People got my face up on their walls. You turn on TV, that's my head. That's sick, man. I used to have a fucking McDonald's costume on. I used to make hamburgers.

*Mark White, the Spin Doctors*

Usually . . . you can do anything you want to do. The idea that you can't walk down the street is in people's mind. You can walk down any street, any time. What you gonna be afraid of, someone coming up to you? In general, it's not that different than it ever was, except you meet people you ordinarily might not meet—you meet some strangers and you talk to 'em for a little while.

*Bruce Springsteen*

I'll tell you how far we've come in the last two years, the real symbol of progress in "Talking Heads." Now I can go 'round to Lou Reed's apartment and I can be rude to him.

*David Byrne*

Some guys don't like it. I don't mind it at all. I was talking to a guy who does what I do the other day, and he said, "I walk down the street and people touch me!" What's the problem?

*Iggy Pop*

In a sense, we're living the myth of the "Dying God," the Icarus myth. The Elvis Presley thing, the Sid Vicious thing. Society wants it and craves it.

*Sting*

I see a lot of people in what is considered the "avant-garde" who are afraid of success. People who go out of their way to be obscure just to be obscure.

*John Oates*

Basically rock stardom comes down to the cut of your trousers.

*David Bowie*

Look, anybody can be a rock star if they put their mind to it. That's what makes rock 'n' roll so great is that somebody like me can actually be a star.

*Elton John*

We're more popular than Jesus Christ now.
*John Lennon, on the Beatles' fame, 1966*

We wouldn't have girlfriends if we weren't in the Ramones.
*Johnny Ramone, the Ramones*

I don't like walking the streets and seeing 30,000 imitations of me.

*Johnny Rotten, 1977*

Our philosophy has always been to do anything to become famous.

*Dee Snider, Twisted Sister*

I drive slow. I'm the guy people are honking at. I'm the only guy that ever took seriously all the stuff they taught in driver's education. To me, the idea of being a rock musician who gets in the car, drives 190 miles an hour, drinks while he drives, and also rides a Harley, is so predictable. That's what you do if you're not sure.

*Chris Isaak*

I got my public life and my private life and they is different.

*Chuck Berry*

Well, to summarize, Big Brother is doing great and I just may be a "star" some day. You know, it's funny. As it gets closer and more probable, being a star is really losing its meaning. But what ever it means I'm ready!

*Janis Joplin, in a letter to her mother, summer 1967*

I'm just not concerned with my popability-profile.

*Chrissie Hynde*

Going to a 7-Eleven in the middle of the night and hearing the clerk whistling one of my songs—that's my idea of a great cover version.

*Warren Zevon*

Fame is like ice cream. It's only bad if you eat too much.
*Mick Jagger, 1982*

I'll tell you true, I've been at the top of the bill and now I'm at the bottom and there's no comparin' 'em. The top beats the bottom every time. At the top you know the people came for you. At the bottom, you're something between the crowd and what they came for, and you gotta work real hard to make it seem worth it to yourself being out there.
*Carl Perkins, 1968*

You get a slight professional twinge when you see any other artist doing well. You say to yourself, "Why not me?"
*Cliff Richard, on the success of the Beatles*

Fame threw me for a loop at first. I learned how to swim with it and turn it around—so you can just throw it in the closet and pick it up when you need it.

*Bob Dylan*

When I was little, I wanted to be famous. I didn't know what it was going to be, I just wanted to be famous. And when I was famous, I just wanted to be good at something.

*Cher*

What goes up comes down and anything that the public embraces, they let go of just as soon. . . .

*Robert Hunter, lyricist, the Grateful Dead*

The postman wants an autograph. The cab driver wants a picture. The waitress wants a handshake. Everyone wants a piece of you.

*John Lennon*

Let's face it, he could have been as big as fucking Jagger, and look at him now . . . it's ridiculous.

*Glen Matlock, ex Sex Pistols, on Johnny Rotten, 1992*

I'm English and I'm gay, so obviously I'm mad. And all celebrities have a period where they lose their marbles.

*Boy George*

# woodstock nation

What they thought was an alternative society was basically a field full of six-foot-deep mud laced with LSD. If that was the world they wanted to live in, then fuck the lot of them.

*Pete Townshend, on Woodstock*

If you look at pictures from the Woodstock movie and see these people squatting in the mud, you'd say, "What are they going to grow up to be? Just look at these guys!" You know, they turned out to be Wall Street. It just goes to show you the flexibility of the human organism that people who would willingly sit in the mud and chant "no rain" periodically between badly amplified rock groups could suddenly turn out to be the ones to run the U.S. economy.

*Frank Zappa*

# that ol' speedway boogie

If Jesus had been there, he would have been crucified.
*Mick Jagger, on Altamont*

Somehow, in America in '69 — I don't know about now, and I never got it before — one got the feeling they really wanted to suck you out.

*Keith Richards*

Don't do free concerts in America.
*Bill Wyman, the Rolling Stones, after being asked the lesson of Altamont*

Sometimes I think the only two people who didn't have a good time there was me and the guy that got killed.
*Mick Jagger, 1975*

I grew up in a tougher part of Jersey than Bruce Springsteen. I wasn't horrified by Altamont, it seemed natural to me. Every high-school dance I went to, somebody was stabbed.
*Patti Smith*

# the devil's music

I think the term heavy metal sucks large quantities of dead penguins' dicks.

*Ted Nugent*

. . . placing truly awesome technical capabilities in the hands of the most musically limited. . . .

*Lester Bangs, critic, on heavy metal*

Heavy metal today is very conservative. You meet so many bands who are really businessmen, approaching it from a business point of view. I think a lot of people can see that it's not a huge put-on when we go onstage. What they see is a bunch of kids having fun playing what we want to play, giving the finger to everyone who wants to interfere.

*Lars Ulrich, Metallica*

There's nothing worse than some heavy metal guy trying to be musically proficient. All I can think of is how much those suckers practice.

*Paul Leary, Butthole Surfers*

Heavy Metal is the totality of existence.

*Rob Halford, Judas Priest*

# disco inferno

I despise it. It's got the one beat, like the military. No creativity. But you gotta go where the money is.

*Carl Gardner, the Coasters, on disco*

Disco music makes it possible to have disco entertainment centers. Disco entertainment centers make it possible for mellow, laid-back, boring kinds of people to meet each other and reproduce.

*Frank Zappa, 1978*

# what's it all mean?

So we've turned a lot of people into fucking nuts by allowing them to misinterpret the words "feed your head." Feed your head doesn't mean take every fucking drug that comes along. Feed your head means read.

*Grace Slick*

It's like a Bob Dylan song that you've loved for years and years, and then you read an interview and he says, "Oh, it's about this dog that was run over in the street." You're like, "What! That song colored and altered my opinion of life for three years. What do you mean it's about a dead dog in the street!"

*Michael Stipe, R.E.M.*

I long ago stopped attempting to "explain" my songs. I much prefer to hear other people do that. I'd rather sort tomatoes. . . .

*David Bowie*

"Layla" was about a woman I felt really deeply about and who turned me down, and I had to pour it out in some way. I mean, her husband is a great musician. It's one of those wife-of-my-best-friend scenes and her husband has been writing great songs for years about her and she still left him.

*Eric Clapton, on "Layla"*

I know who the Sad-Eyed Lady of the Lowland really is, no matter who he says it's about.

*Joan Baez*

---

# turn me on, dead man

It was a hot day. I had sandals on, and I kicked them off. Big deal.

*Paul McCartney, dispelling the "Paul is dead" theory based in part on his being pictured barefoot on the cover of the* Abbey Road *album*

I said "Cranberry Sauce." That's all I said. Some people like ping-pong, other people like digging over graves. Some people will do anything rather than be here now.

*John Lennon, 1980, asked to explain the line in "I Am the Walrus" that sounds like "I buried Paul"*

I hate people asking me what I mean in my songs, 'cause it's none of their business. I also hate being asked, "How do I feel being a woman in rock."

*Sinead O'Connor*

A lot of people come up and say, "Oh, you are speaking to me, you are telling my life story on this song." I'll say, "Give me a break," but it's true! I listen to it, it is my life and it feels like I'm listening to someone else sing it.

*Paul Westerberg, the Replacements*

"Runaround Sue" was written about a chick named Dolores. She was the neighborhood whore. At the time I couldn't get anything to rhyme with it, other than Lavoris and clitoris, so we wrote it about Sue.

*Dion*

I'm obsessed with truth and how the futile scramble for material things obscures our possible path to understanding ourselves, each other and the universe in ways that will make human life more fulfilling for all human beings. That's what "Dark Side of the Moon" is about, and what most of my records have been about.

*Roger Waters*

To me, "Mighty Quinn" is about the five Perfect Masters of the age, the best of all being Meher Baba of course. To Dylan, it's probably about gardening, or the joys of placing dog shit in the garbage to foul up Alan J. Weberman.

*Pete Townshend*

Sometimes I'm not sure what a lot of our songs are about.

*Jim Kerr, Simple Minds*

I read in the paper Anne Murray said, "Sometimes you get a good meaningful song and sometimes you get a piece of crap. I defy anyone but the songwriter to tell me what 'Daydream Believer' is all about."

*John Stewart*

People want to know what the inner meaning of "Mr. Kite" was. There wasn't any. I just did it. I shoved a lot of words together then shoved some noise on. I just did it. I didn't dig that song when I wrote it. I didn't believe in it when I was doing it. But nobody will believe it. They don't want to. They want it to be important. People think the Beatles know what's going on. We don't. We're just doing it.

*John Lennon*

Q: Did you ever know a girl named Maybelline?
A: No. The only Maybelline I knew was the name of a cow. . . .

*Chuck Berry*

I put a lot into my lyrics. Not all my stuff is meant to be scrutinized, though. Things like "Black Dog" are blatant let's-do-it-in-the-bath type things, but they make their point just the same. People listen. Otherwise, you might as well sing the menu from the Continental Hyatt House.

*Robert Plant*

It began to get to me. I had done everything that I could as the old Alice and I was tired of playing that same monster over and over. . . . When you get older, maybe you just want to be respected a little more or something. It just got to the point where I said to myself, "Alice, school's out!" Do you know where I got that line originally? Everyone who heard it on the album thought it meant something else, but it was from these guys, the Bowery Boys. . . . I was watching one of their old movies one day and Leo Gorcey was telling Huntz Hall he better smarten up, you know? He says, "Satch, you big dummy—school's out!"

*Alice Cooper*

Some people have accused us of being bitter for writing "Rock and Roll Star." It's no more bitter than "Positively Fourth Street." In fact, it isn't nearly as bitter as that. We were thumbing through a teen magazine and looking at all the unfamiliar faces and couldn't help but think, "Wow! What happened? All of a sudden here's everybody and his brother and his sister-in-law and his mother and his pet bull-frog singing rock and roll." So we wrote "So You Want to Be a Rock and Roll Star" to the audience who is going to be potential rock and roll stars, who were going to be, who would like to be . . . and some did realize their goals.

*Roger McGuinn, the Byrds*

I don't know. It's sort of an epistle to ambiguity. "This is a song of hope." That's what I said, that's what it is. And I saw a bustle in the hedgerow last Friday on the Welsh border!

*Robert Plant, on the meaning of "Stairway to Heaven"*

Q: What's the line that comes after "Blinded by the the light . . . "?

A: Woke up with a doozie in the middle of the night. — *Lisa*

Wrapped up in a noose; got a rubber-ended knife. — *Jaina*

Wound up with a moose in the rolling thunder night. — *what I thought Eric Baecht said*

Soaked it up like a douche in the rinnie-ninnie night. — *what Eric really said*

Revved up like a tooth. You know, the motor and the bite. — *Scott Derrr*

Roped up like a goose in the shimmy-shimmy night. — *Alex Behr*

Fuck up with a contusion and give your plants the blight. — *Matt Jasper*

And little early burly gave my anus curly whirly and asked me if I needed a ride. — *Rachel*

Why do you want to know? Why do you want to know, I'm asking you. I know it. Wrapped up like a crooner . . . what is the word? Loser? I like Manfred Mann's early stuff, but . . . wrapped up like . . . tell me! — *A man in a bar from the music 'zine* Rollerderby

# comfortably numb

Yeah, well, I don't know. I've been round and round with the drug thing. People are always wanting me to take a stand on drugs, and I can't. To me, it's so relativistic, and it's also very personal. A person's relationship to drugs is like their relationship to sex. I mean, who is standing on such high ground that they can say: "You're cool. You're not."

*Jerry Garcia*

What I find difficult to take seriously now is some groups we have in England who are pretending to be on drugs. That's a very strange thing. Perhaps they're aware that doing the same drugs that achieved a certain effect in 1967 won't achieve the same effect now, because circumstances are so different.

*Elvis Costello, 1991*

To think that one kid would do heroin because I did it is like ten points for me going to hell, you know what I mean? Some things just need to be in the closet.

*Courtney Love, Hole*

The path of excess leads to a dirt plot in a foreign land that people pour booze on and put out cigarettes on.

*Axl Rose, Guns N' Roses, after visiting*
*Jim Morrison's grave in Paris*

Excess was the order of the day, and he was beyond the ordinary excess.

*Terry Melcher, producer, on Gram Parsons*

While I was a junkie I learned to ski and made *Exile on Main Street*.

*Keith Richards*

Our story is that basically we had it all and then we threw it all away. I snorted my airplane. I snorted my Porsche. I snorted my house.

*Steven Tyler, Aerosmith*

Music is a safe type of high. It's more the way it's supposed to be. That's where highness came, I guess, from anyway. It's nothing but rhythm and motion.

*Jimi Hendrix*

There's something to be said for taking drugs and being at your best because when it works well—that one time out of 10—you transcend so that the light is coming in from heaven into the top of your head and out the end of your sticks.

*Pete Thomas, the Attractions*

I saw Keith Richards and he hugged me and said, "Nice one Phil, you took care of Gram"—I nearly said "You're next!"

The shape he was in you shouldn't smoke around him, he might go up.

*Phil Kaufman, a close friend of Gram Parsons,*
*entrusted with burning Parsons' dead body,*
*a promise he kept, 1981*

Drugs handle people, not the other way around.

*Cher*

I don't have a drug problem, I have a police problem.

*Keith Richards, 1978*

You can't play while you're tripping. The guitar turns into a three-foot piece of rubber, and your fingers go right through the strings.

*David Crosby*

There was so much acid during the '60s that it was very easy for large numbers of people to think they had seen God as soon as the Beatles went boom, boom, boom, you know? So that particular chemical made a lot of really peculiar things possible in terms of musical sales. And since the status of that drug has been wearing off, and other things are taking its place—notably wine and beer—you have a different kind of audience mentality.

*Frank Zappa, 1978*

In fact I never learned any diplomacy at all until I started smoking pot.

*Phil Lesh, Grateful Dead*


A coke problem is almost part of the package for stardom, you know. Lennon had it, Keith had it. In a way you got lulled into it. I'm glad I'm the way I am now, came out of it with most of my mind intact.

*John Taylor, Duran Duran*


Okay, I admit I'm a bit of a speed freak, but I never touch smack. Besides, people who like smack also like Lou Reed, and that can't be anything in its favour.

*Lemmy, Motorhead, 1972*

# punk

Punk is musical freedom. It's saying, doing and playing what you want. In Webster's terms, nirvana means freedom from pain, suffering and the external world, and that's pretty close to my definition of punk rock.

*Kurt Cobain, Nirvana*

I think punk rock was rather like taking the mirror and smashing it and watching the shards displace.

*Billy Idol*

Punk changed the business, but only temporarily. English pop music is still about trivia and homosexuals, isn't it?!!

*John Lydon, 1983*

One day at the breakfast table my daughter was listening to the music, and I noticed this punk look about her.

*Pam Howar, president of the PMRC*

Punk will never die until something more dangerous replaces it.

*Jello Biafra, the Dead Kennedys*

Of course it's false but it's easier not to question those myths. To question it threatens the whole bullshit rock 'n' roll dream. We're real rebels—rebels limited to a verse-chorus-verse format, the same guitar lines, the same stage antics. All that changes are the fucking clothes and hairdo's.

*John Lydon, asked if it's a false belief that*
*one needs conflict to create*

When I first heard about punk back in '77 I'd been waiting for six years to hear that kind of commitment: to hear some geezer hit a drum as if all he wanted to do in his life was hit a drum. And to me it was all a great political statement. Because the movement that I'd been a part of went off course.

*Robert Fripp*

I mean, the first time I ever saw John Rotten, I was really shocked, 'cause I had never actually seen the whole thing in person. He sort of crystallized the whole punk attitude, and there's no doubt about it, the guy had amazing charisma.

*Roger Taylor, Queen*

The same thing happened to punk rock. When punk came along, for all its efforts to turn itself into the ultimate nauseating hair ball, the industry just extruded some new and different tubes and sucked it down—much to the benefit of popular music. That's why we've got R.E.M. and everything else I can stand to listen to these days—because the industry swallowed the punk hair ball and actually digested it.

*William Gibson, writer, comparing the fate*
*of cyberpunk to punk*

I like punk. I'm not that into it. . . . I regard it as another style with good fashion and a good attitude.

*Paul McCartney*

Nobody's gonna like you guys, but I'll have you back.
*Hilly Kristal, owner of CBGB, to the Ramones after their audition*

# england's dreaming

Well, I'm not pleased at Johnny Rotten, who says all nasty things about me. I know that he feels he has to because I'm, along with the Queen, you know, one of the best things England's got. Me and the Queen.

*Mick Jagger*

There is no doubt in my mind that the Sex Pistols were England's greatest contribution to rock 'n' roll, well over and above the Rolling Stones or the Beatles.

*Malcolm McLaren*

# great rock 'n' roll moments on television

We were miming to the record and Mick was singing live, and when he came to the line, "Trying to make some girl" they beeped it so it came out, "Trying to BEEP some girl," which made it so much worse because everybody's vivid imaginations were trying to figure out what he really said. [Laughs] "What did he say?" "Did he say . . . fuck?" In the end it kind of helped our image in a way. [Laughs] I mean, it's still talked about now, right?

> *Bill Wyman, on the Rolling Stones performing*
> *"Satisfaction" on the Ed Sullivan Show*

Grundy:         I'm told that that group [referring to a just-aired clip of the Sex Pistols in concert] have received 40,000 pounds from a record company. Doesn't that seem . . . err . . . to be slightly opposed to their anti-materialistic view of life?

Glen Matlock: No. The more the merrier.

Grundy:         Really?

Matlock:        Oh yeah.

Grundy:         Tell me more then.

Steve Jones:   We've fuckin' spent it, ain't we?

Grundy:         I don't know. Have you?

Matlock:        Yeah. It's all gone.

Grundy:      Really?

Matlock:     Down the boozer.

> *from a transcript of the December 1976 appearance*
> *by the Sex Pistols on Britain's "Today" program*
> *hosted by Bill Grundy*

If you want to know the exact moment that rock 'n' roll started, it was right then.

> *Quincy Jones, on Elvis Presley's appearance on the*
> *"Dorsey Brothers Stage Show" television program,*
> *January 28, 1956*

Why are you a Sting?

> *Sam Donaldson, to Sting, on ABC's "Nightline," 1983,*
> *live from the site of the US Festival in California*

We're all heads.

> *Dave Hall, guitarist for the 13th Floor Elevators,*
> *responding to the question, "Are you ahead of*
> *your time?" from Dick Clark on "American*
> *Bandstand," October 31, 1967*

# to grunge or not to grunge

To me the soul of rock 'n' roll is mistakes. Mistakes and making mistakes work for you. In general, music that's flawless is usually uninspired.

*Paul Westerberg, the Replacements*

I hate sloppiness of any kind!

*Brian Jones, the Rolling Stones, 1966*

Long, flat expanses of professionalism bother me. I'd rather have a band that could explode at any time. And I think that's what people like, too: soul and expression and real fire and emotion more than perfection.

*Neil Young*

# i get excitement at your feet

Trying to tart the music business up is getting nearer to what the kids themselves are like. Because what I find, if you want to talk in terms of rock, a lot depends on sensationalism and the kids themselves are more sensational than the stars themselves.

*David Bowie*

Many people think I'm from outer space. Actually, I'm from New Jersey. It's hard to communicate with someone who thinks you're an alien. I feel I have to prove I'm normal by buying them a beer and playing a video game with them.

*David Byrne*

This shit scares me sometimes. The way kids are into us, the way the adults hate us. Nobody gets it. It's amazing. Shit, dude! It's all right off TV.

*Tom Araya, Slayer, reading his fan mail*

The kids want misery and death. They want threatening noises because that shakes you out of your apathy.

*John Lydon*

Those weird people on the street—every hundredth weirdest one has a Steely Dan record at home.

*Walter Becker, Steely Dan*

In some instances, it gets a little crazy, sort of like a lesbian Beatlemania.

*k.d. lang, on her concerts*

Last year I was feeling real depressed and suicidal. And I received a fan letter from a guy who had heard that I was down. I didn't even know him, but he really made me believe that my songs meant something to him and that he would really be missing something if I didn't write any more. That really helped pull me out of it. I'd like to think the people that we mean something to, we mean a great deal to.

*Peter Holsapple, the dB's*

American kids can't just go and listen to music, can they? They have to get stoned. Or they have to get drunk. They can't just go and have fun. And you get the violent ones. . . . They're not interested in the music, and it's a shame, because it always spoils it for everybody else—the good people.

*Bill Wyman, the Rolling Stones*

Broken windows, smashed hotel rooms, this and the other is no big deal. The death of some kid who's going to a concert to have a great time and probably waited for months, saved his money, took the train, and then to get pushed down from behind by 120,000 people and no one had the decency to help you up, that was your last day on earth—that's heavy.

*Slash, Guns N' Roses, on the death of a fan*

People look at musicians through different colored glasses. You meet a girl backstage and there's a lot of fantasy involved as to what they think you are and what their being with you makes them, and you have to remember your lines. If you blow your lines the fantasy collapses.

*David Lee Roth, Van Halen, 1981*

I sit out in the parking lot for an hour after a concert and talk to people—sometimes for two hours, sometimes for so long it irritates everyone else, and they're like "Natalie, let's go!" and I'm like "I haven't talked to everyone yet!"

*Natalie Merchant, 10,000 Maniacs*

Being on the stage and looking at the audience, one thing is clear; we know better who the audience is. You know we really do. They don't really know who we are. They don't really know that we're just shit like them.

*Pete Townshend*

I'm cocky. I know I can sing. I give an impression of all this strength. Maybe that's why the lesbian crowd likes me and the gay boys spill their guts to me. I act like I'm ready to kick anyone's ass who's in my way.

*Etta James*

When my record first hit, a lot of people thought I was black—and a lot of people thought I was a woman.

*Johnnie Ray, on his early 1950s hit*

I'm still not sure who my audience is. I have a terrible feeling they might be yuppies

*Billy Bragg*

The dream of my life has always been to be the reason that someone else bought a $35.00 ticket like they do for Daryl's concerts. Still, I get a kick out of being the star's friend, and Daryl doesn't forget where he started. So, I don't have 125,000 people screaming for me at the Spectrum. Daryl can't cut toenails.

*Paul Fogel, Pennsylvania podiatrist who sang with Daryl Hall in a street-corner style vocal group in college*

You give them a lot of fantastic energy and they eat it and spit it out. They're like loving vampires or something.

*Patti Smith, on her audience*

Our audience is like people who like licorice. Not everybody likes licorice, but the people who like licorice really like licorice.

*Jerry Garcia*

If you're lucky, people like something you do early and something you do just before you drop dead. That's as many pats on the back as you should expect.

*Warren Zevon*

# talking to the fans

Clap if we played something you came to hear.
*Bob Dylan, to a concert audience, 1981*

You cowboys are all faggots.
*Sid Vicious, to an audience in Texas on the Sex Pistols' first and only tour of America, 1978*

We're really nervous, but love you all, man, 'cause this is very groovy. Monterey is very groovy. This is something, man. This is our generation, all you people. We're all together. Dig yourselves. It's really groovy.

*Michael Bloomfield, the Electric Flag, prior to the band's very first performance at the Monterey Pop Festival, 1967*

I honestly think I understand the fans. I remember following Johnnie Ray around Liverpool. He went into a restaurant, ordered a meal and was eating, and I said to a friend who was with me, "Look, he's eating like a real person." So I remember what it's like from the other side. Even at the rehab center, where the people were great to me, everyone had their one question about the Beatles. Everybody gets to ask one.

*Ringo Starr*

If you get a clever audience, they can make you collapse.

*Alvin Lee, Ten Years After*

The Fillmore East has a light show because the audience has eyes and the musicians don't always know it.

*Kip Cohen, lights technician, Fillmore East*

"Please Mick. Chew some and send it back."
*a fan letter sent to Mick Jagger that included a pack of gum and a stamped, addressed return envelope*

If I had my way, I'd play for nothing but 17-year-old girls. They don't care how old the music is, or who wrote it. They like to dance. Nothing makes me more nervous than people sitting there just staring at me when I play.

*George Thorogood*

I believe that the life of a rock and roll band will last as long as you can look down into the audience and can see yourself and your audience looks up at you and can see themselves. . . . The biggest gift your fans can give you is just treatin' you like a human being, because anything else dehumanizes you. If the price of fame is that you have to be isolated from the people you write for, then that's too fuckin' high a price to pay.

*Bruce Springsteen*

The audience has to realize that it's basically theater and you're kind of role-playing. And at the end of the song it's over. So don't come to my house and tell me it's not over.

*Richard Thompson*

Prison audiences are the best audiences in the world.

*Johnny Cash*

But I know what the fans mean, and we try to please everybody. A lot of times when we're on stage there is a terrific temptation to go further out but then you hold back because some people aren't going to undertstand.

*Eric Clapton, 1968*

And then Jerry Wexler comes creeping out of the woodwork and he says, "My son's in college and he has all of your records." I said, "Gee, I hope it hasn't affected his work!"

*Frank Zappa*

When you are listening to a rock and roll song the way you listen to "Jumping Jack Flash," or something similar, that's the way you should really spend your whole life.

*Pete Townshend*

They don't want the discipline of the home, and yet they want the security. And the only thing that will give them security is to give them what they want. It's very weird. And that takes growing up.

*Spencer Dryden, Jefferson Airplane, on rock audiences*

Being the focus of what amounts to a quasi-religious cult is just weird. I don't really change what I do that much.

*Bob Weir, the Grateful Dead*

They're the people who are down in front and insist upon being there every show. You know, so for us, our experience with the shows now is that we know these people pretty intimately, you know. We look down there and now if there's somebody new there we notice them.

*Jerry Garcia, explaining a Deadhead subset, the "railers"*

The Grateful Dead is different. It gets into your bones. The music is through my feet, up my body, to the sky.

*a deaf Deadhead*

For years I kept hearing that people wanted another "Blue" or "Court and Spark," but it's not as if someone went into their record collections and stole them. If I gave them more of that, they'd be bored.

*Joni Mitchell*

When no one listens to your music, it's lonelier than masturbation. Now, I love masturbation, but not as a musical style.

*Warren Cuccurullo, Duran Duran*

A lot of those same kids sitting there, pumping their arms in the air, are the same kids that would've beaten me up seven years ago, the same kids that wouldn't have let me into their parties. If the alternative world is only made up of white, upper-middle-class, good-looking people, what kind of world is that? I'm trying to understand it more.

*Weiland, Stone Temple Pilots*

It was the most we could do to get through a song, presenting each one in another dramatic light—a catastrophic or plaintive or tragic light. When you play in the dark with your back to the audience, that's what the attitude is. It's no wonder we never knew who our audiences were—we never looked at them.

*John Cale, the Velvet Underground*

Our initial following, the club-goers, had gone away, and been replaced by a teenage girl following, and then you last just as long as your poster lasts on the back of the wardrobe door. As soon as that gets a bit peeled and curly at the corners, as far as they're concerned you're a bit peeled and curly at the corners. And that's it—down the back of the sofa.

*Simon Le Bon, Duran Duran*

In the '60s they all treated us like we were great philosopher gods that knew all the answers. We were the flying saucers of the '60s, if you know what I mean. People were looking for someone to tell them how to run their lives.

*Paul Kantner, Jefferson Airplane/Starship*

# it's just a shot away
# (it's just a kiss away)

Greetings and welcome Rolling Stones, our comrades in the desparate [sic] battle against the maniacs who hold power. . . . We will play your music in rock-'n'-roll marching bands as we tear down the jails and free the prisoners, as we tear down the State schools and free the students, as we tear down the military bases and arm the poor, as we tattoo BURN BABY BURN! on the bellies of the wardens and generals and create a new society from the ashes of our fires. . . . THE ROLLING STONES ARE THAT WHICH SHALL BE! LYNDON JOHNSON — THE YOUTH OF CALIFORNIA DEDICATES ITSELF TO YOUR DESTRUCTION! ROLLING STONES — THE YOUTH OF CALIFORNIA HEARS YOUR MESSAGE! LONG LIVE THE REVOLUTION!!!

*from a street poster welcoming the Rolling Stones on their first tour of the West Coast of the United States*

The TV will edit this out, like they'll cut all the groovy things Country Joe said. But I'm gonna say it anyway: John F. Kennedy was shot from a number of different positions by a number of guns. The facts have been suppressed, witnesses killed, and this is your country, ladies and gentlemen.

*David Crosby, in the introduction that probably sealed his fate as a Byrd, at the Monterey Pop festival, 1967*

It would be wrong for me to say, "Yes, we can change the world with a song"—but every time I try writing, that's where I'm at. I'm not stupid. I'm aware of the futility of rock 'n' roll music. But I'm also aware of its power.

*Bono*


And, in fact, I don't think we even see ourselves as messengers. The message is already there, very clearly. If you stop for a moment and close your eyes and listen to the thundering demons, the horses of the toxic apocalypse, you're going to know.

*Peter Garrett, Midnight Oil*


There are some people who want us to go around singing revolutionary songs for the next 35 years. Well, that's not now. That was then. To do it over again would be like listening to Rudy Vallee with that big megaphone. It gets very boring during the age of microphones.

*Paul Kantner, Jefferson Airplane/Starship*


I think you have to make a distinction, not between art and politics, but between art and propaganda. Politics is a part of life, and you would be ignoring a whole aspect of life by leaving it out of songs.

*Bruce Cockburn*

Who wants politics in music? I find politics the single most uninspiring, unemotional, insensitive activity on this planet.

*Adam Ant*

What's interesting about rock 'n' roll is that its truly radical aspect occurs at the level of sound. "Tutti Frutti" is far more revolutionary than Lennon's "Woman Is the Nigger of the World," and the sound of Dylan's voice changed more people's ideas about the world than his political message did.

*Robert Ray, the Vulgar Boatmen*

Q: How do you feel about people who combine music and politics?
A: Buncha fuckin' idiots.

*Jerry Lee Lewis*

Let me tell you about politics. Have you ever heard my wrestling scenario? It goes like this: The arenas are always packed for Hulk Hogan. The crowd yells, "Oh look at the macho man! Look at his scar!" Those same people vote.

*Ice-T*

I'm interested in anything about revolt, disorder, chaos, especially activity that appears to have no meaning. It seems to me to be the road toward freedom.

*Jim Morrison*

To me music is always just love, I guess, just happiness. Singin' a happy song. I don't think politics should enter into music. When it does, it makes me a little queasy. 'Cause I don't dig politics that much.

*Marty Balin, Jefferson Airplane*

I'm a revolutionary and, yes, it's a burden.

*Madonna*

This is why the Iron Curtain went down. It was jeans and rock and roll that took that wall down in the long run. It wasn't all those atomic weapons and that facing down and big bullshit. What finally crumbled it was the fuckin' music, man. You cannot stop it. It is the most subversive thing.

*Keith Richards*

We want to be the band to dance to when the bomb drops.

*Simon Le Bon, Duran Duran, 1984*

When the underground thing was happening, the players would take insane stands for what they believed. The fact of the matter is that it is dangerous, because a guy of 25 who has spent most of his adult life in the rock 'n' roll industry is not wise to the world's problems. To be a people's prophet is a dangerous thing.

*Greg Lake, Emerson, Lake and Palmer*

I'm glad you have new records; not long ago, I wanted to write you to get hold of "The Wall."

*Vaclav Havel, in a letter from prison to his wife, Olga*

# playing in the band

. . . I play bass in a band, man. That's all I think about. I'm
not trying to be false modest or any of that shit. That's it. I
play in a band I love. Legendary? Fuck that. Legendary's like
Hemingway, O.K.? We're just a rock 'n' roll band and that's
all there is to it. . . .

*Duff McKagan, Guns N' Roses*

They're gonna look back at the Beatles and the Stones and all
those guys are relics. The days when those bands were just
all men will be on the newsreels, you know. . . . That's
gonna be the joke in the future, not a couple singing together
or living and working together. It's all right when you're 16,
17, 18 to have male companions and idols, OK? It's tribal
and it's gangs and it's fine. But when it continues and you're
still doing it when you're 40, that means you're still 16 in the
head.

*John Lennon, 1980*

Sometimes you can put together four or five really talented
musicians and get a really terrible band. Nothing. And then
sometimes you can put together four or five sort of mediocre
musicians and get a great band. That's rock and roll.

*Sammy (Llanas) BoDean, the BoDeans*

Being the new keyboardist in this band is like being the new guy in 'Nam.

> *Vince Welnick, latest keyboardist for*
> *the Grateful Dead*

I'd always had problems getting laid before I was in a band. Now, I don't understand—but it's great.

> *Bob Geldof, the Boomtown Rats*

Being realistic, The Sex Pistols were a total failure, when you consider how much we had going for us, and how we blew it.

> *Glen Matlock, ex Sex Pistols*

When you're in a rock band, bragging about sexual conquests is like bragging about turning on the faucet and finding water.

> *Paul Stanley, Kiss*

It's a very unusual thing to be in a band like this. It's like being in a street gang. And it's all very well being in a street gang when you're 16, but it's bloody weird when you're 32.

> *The Edge, U2*

Being in a rock and roll band is very much like having a Sherman tank around you at all times. And I took advantage of that. It's just the same as the protection that was offered to Keith Moon; if he'd been, say, a highly paid accountant and drove people's cars into a swimming pool, he wouldn't have gotten off the way he did. He was allowed the freedom to be goofy and hedonistic: let's fuck off until we die.

*Grace Slick*

We want a guy who's amiable and doesn't cause any trouble.
*Mick Jagger, on picking a new bassist*
*to replace Bill Wyman*

Look at someone like Jimi Hendrix. I mean, he had a couple of boys with him but they weren't a band in the way we've come to know each other over the years. If there's anything that's stopped us from blowing our loudspeakers, it's probably each other.

*Keith Richards*

I've always liked to be in a band. I do like bands, and any occasion I can have to be in a band is good fun. I like the teamwork.

*Paul McCartney*

I've done that hundreds of times. I've had like 17 bands. I hate it, personally. I'd much rather just play guitar and let the other guy lose all the money.

*Slim Dunlap, ex Replacements, on leading a band*

. . . but when it came down to getting hold of a singer, it was either going to be Steve Winwood or Steve Marriot. Finally it came down to Marriot. He was contacted and the reply came back from his manager's office: "How would you like to have a group with no fingers, boys?" Or words to that effect.

*Jimmy Page, Led Zeppelin, on the influence managers*
*had in putting bands together during*
*the early 1960s*

Any group that really gets along has to be suspect.
*Andy Summers, the Police*

Each band has a finite life in terms of the number of gigs played.
*Sterling Morrison, the Velvet Underground*

It's funny, but you've got all these young bands coming up that, in the words of Dee-Dee Ramone, consider that "a song is three chords and a grudge." I mean there's definitely more and more pissed-off kids.
*Tina Weymouth, Talking Heads*

# idiot wind

You can't ban things just because there's a couple of lunatics out there, committing suicide after they hear a Judas Priest record. You know, people aren't going to go into really hurtful sex acts because they go to a Mapplethorpe exhibition. It's just not the way it works.

*Lou Reed*

Senator Hawkins: Do you make a profit from sales of rock records?

Mr. Zappa:     Yes.

Senator Hawkins: So you do make a profit from the sales of rock records?

Mr. Zappa:     Yes.

Senator Hawkins: Thank you. I think that statement tells the story to this committee. Thank you.

*from the testimony of Frank Zappa before*
*the Senate Commerce Committee hearings*
*on record labeling, 1985*

Illegal. They are really out to make rock and roll illegal. Really, it would be illegal to play the goddamn music. That's the basic drive behind the whole thing. They are just scared of that rhythm. That disturbs them. Every sound's vibration has a certain effect on you. And there is nothing you can do about it. Certainly, every sound has an effect on the body and the effects of a good backbeat make these people shiver in their boots. So you are fighting some primeval fear that you can't even rationalize because it has to do with chromosomes and exploding genes.

*Keith Richards*


There are more love songs than anything else. If songs could make you do something, we'd all love one another.

*Frank Zappa*


The Duran Duran songs were demonic, and Tina Turner and Mick Jagger did their bumping, grinding duet . . . face-to-face, belly-to-belly. . . . It's hard to look at something like that and think, "I'm going to send money to starving kids."

*Pat Boone, on Live Aid*


They seem to think that if you sing about something, then some kid is automatically going to go out and copy it. If that was the case, every teenager in America would have a gun and go round shooting people after watching Miami Vice. It's insane. And anyway, how many people you know can afford a guillotine?

*Alice Cooper, 1986*


Often we would say that a particular number was a protest song with a good message. For instance, we'd tell them that "Paint It Black" was about discrimination and race relations, or that "Lady Madonna" was about a woman standing in an unemployment line.

> *Grisha Dimant, former Soviet rocker,*
> *on how he duped government censors*

The kids accept almost any form of rock and roll, even the lowest and most distasteful. . . . It seems to encourage sloppy clothes that become the accepted uniform. It's one step from Fascism!

> *Mitch Miller*

I would say that a buzz saw blade between the guy's legs on the album cover is a good indication that it's not for little Johnny.

> *Frank Zappa, commenting on the album cover for*
> *WASP's* I F-✳-C-K Like a Beast *in testimony before*
> *the Senate Commerce Committee hearings*
> *on record labeling, 1985*

The effect of rock and roll in young people is to turn them into devil worshippers; to stimulate self-expression through sex; to provoke lawlessness, impair nervous stability and destroy the sanctity of marriage. It is an evil influence on the youth of our country.

> *Reverend Albert Carter, minister of*
> *the Pentecostal Church, 1956*

Uh-oh, I think I exposed myself out there . . .
*Jim Morrison, March 1969*


They wouldn't know the Antichrist if he hit them across the face with a wet kipper.
*Joe Strummer, the Clash, on a demonstration*
*denouncing punks as the Antichrist*


And that Jerry Falwell . . . he can kiss my ass twice. . . .
*Bruce Springsteen, in concert, 1988*


Ma'am, ah'm not tryin' to be sexy. Ah didn't have any idear of trying to sell sex. It's just my way of expressin' how I feel when I move around. It's all leg movement. Ah don't do no-thin' with my body.
*Elvis Presley, to a reporter early in his career*

# start me up!

Chuck was my man. He was the one that made me say as a teenager, "I want to play guitar, Jesus Christ!" And then suddenly I had a focal point, but not that I was naive enough, even at that age, to expect it to pan out. But at least I had something to go for, some way to channel the energies that you have at that age. And definitely with rock and roll, you have to start somewhere around then.

*Keith Richards*

When I was nine, I got *With the Beatles,* and my grandma bought me a honky old drum and an old cymbal. That's it isn't it; what more is there? A drum, a cymbal and *With the Beatles.* Has the world really come on much further?

*Pete Thomas, the Attractions*

Q: How'd you start on drums?
A: Jesus Christ, I think I got a free drum kit in a packet of corn flakes. Ah-Ha-Ha-Ha-Ha-Ha-Ha-Ha-Ha!

*Keith Moon*

My first pop idol was Nancy Sinatra. Go-go boots, miniskirt, blond hair, fake eyelashes—she was cool.

*Madonna*

The first records my mom brought home that I was really knocked out by were "Hound Dog" and Haley's "ABC Boogie." They changed my life, I couldn't believe it. I heard Little Richard and Jerry Lee Lewis and that was it. I didn't ever want to be anything else.

*Elton John*

How did I decide to form the Byrds? I saw the Beatles, that's why. Bang. That's the answer. That's all. That was enough. It turned me on, you know?

*Roger McGuinn, the Byrds*

If I hadn't heard the Rolling Stones back in 1964, I wouldn't be playing guitar today. I thought they were really the last word, but then I found out about the people they called their idols: Howlin' Wolf, Robert Johnson, Muddy Waters, Chuck Berry—those guys. That was all the hint I needed. After the Stones turned me on to the real thing, I completely forgot about Mick Jagger.

*George Thorogood*

The thing was that you could imagine that you could be smart like Wittgenstein by just thinking hard enough but Elvis had it. It was almost spiritual, a kind of grace, a kind of innate ruling of the world.

*Richard Hell*

The Rosetta Stone of rock 'n' roll. When I heard that record, all of a sudden it clicked: "This is what I want to do."

*Chris Isaak, on the* Sun Sessions

It was the first rock 'n' roll I'd heard, to my ears—'cause you're too young to understand the Rolling Stones when you're five.

*Paul Westerberg, the Replacements, on hearing
the Sex Pistols for the first time*

## six turned out to be nine

I first heard Hendrix when I was driving my mother's station wagon in New Hampshire. There aren't too many radio stations there—you just got bits and pieces through the static. I heard "Purple Haze," and I thought, "Now we're getting Martian radio."

*Joe Perry, Aerosmith*

I started playing it, and my son said, "Dad, what's that?" I said, "Well, that's God."

*Robert Plant, describing his fourteen-year-old
son's reaction to his playing a Jimi Hendrix
best-of collection*

A: Naw, I didn't sing much when I was a kid. As a matter of fact, in Sunday school when everyone was singing "Onward Christian Soldiers," I was singing "Home on the Range."

Q: Why?

A: It was my favorite song.

*Lowell George, Little Feat*

We were always listening to music . . . early rock, guys like Little Richard, Elvis, Bill Haley, Buddy Holly . . . we always wanted to be in a rock and roll band—but we didn't think it was possible.

*Johnny Ramone, the Ramones*

That Elvis, man, he is all there is. There ain't no more. Everything starts and ends with him. He wrote the book.

*Bruce Springsteen*

Black Sabbath. We've taken everything we know from Black Sabbath.

*Ben Shepherd, Soundgarden*

# keef!

You can't drink with him, but you can write with him. He's totally mystified by music, like a kid. He finds great joy in it, and madness and abandon. He looks at the guitar, and his eyes get all big and he starts shakin' his head. He's made out of something that music likes to be around.

*Charlie Watts, the Rolling Stones,*
*on Keith Richards*

There are many side roads and back streets to rock 'n' roll, and most of us get lost down them at times. But I found Keith to be very much on the main road. He was still in love with music. You can see that all his infamy and fortune don't matter much to him. When he puts on the guitar, lines disappear from his face.

*Bono, on Keith Richards*

# some stuff for people who can't read

Rock criticism shouldn't be "I like these lyrics because of this" or "It's got a good beat, because I can dance to it"—it should encompass the magic that rock and roll is. The best rock criticism that I see makes me want to go out and buy a record, even if I don't get a really clear picture of what the record is all about.

*Peter Buck, R.E.M.*

Rock journalism is people who can't write interviewing people who can't talk for people who can't read.

*Frank Zappa*

What do I think about critics? I think they're a bunch of shits.

*Freddie Mercury, Queen*

Some of them just don't get it, of course, but when teenagers do get something, they understand it more deeply than the critics who are writing about it. The critics have to look to the teenagers. Teenagers are the validation of rock 'n' roll.

*David Lowery, Camper Van Beethoven*

There are some forms that simply shouldn't have critics. It's just too much for the little form to bear. Movies, for example, and, of course, rock 'n' roll.

*Fran Liebowitz, writer*

Journalists are sometimes pretty dense, and they imagine they're writing for people who are as dense as they are. They come to our gigs and then start writing about brawling Paddies, which is nonsense. I read something in an American magazine about our tours in England being a succession of drunken fistfights. That's complete nonsense.

*Philip Chevron, the Pogues*

I can't actually play any instrument properly. I can't read music. And here's the *New York Times* calling me the new George Gershwin. . . .

*Elvis Costello*

Q: Do you want to be immortal through your songs?
A: No, I'd like to be immortal through my body.

*Rickie Lee Jones*

They're critics because they have no talent to play music.

*Robert Plant*

Rock critics like Elvis Costello because rock critics look like Elvis Costello.

*attributed to David Lee Roth by critic Lisa Robinson*

It's difficult for me to imagine a more pretentious occupation than that of professional critic, a task commonly inherited by the failed actor, the failed musician and . . . the failed writer.

*Sting*

Bad reviews don't bother me. But a lot of these critics are looking for art. The thing that got me was, people who are looking for art in rock and roll or pop are looking for something that either doesn't or shouldn't exist there. An artist is a guy with a beret who sits in a park and paints pictures, and he starves in a garret somewhere.

*Billy Joel*

Elvis escaped the guilt of the blues—the guilt that is at the heart of the world the blues and country music give us—because he was able to replace the sense that men and women were trapped by fate and by their sins with a complex of emotions that were equally strong and distinctive.

*Greil Marcus, writer*

Greil Marcus, I think it was, who said, "Biggest waste of one of the finest voices of the twentieth century. . . . " or something like that. When I read that, I felt, "Geez, he's absolutely right." 'Cause I was making some horrible records. I'd bastardized my art. I'd made records like "Do Ya Think I'm

Sexy?" and "Love Touch." Nothing more than just horrible pop songs.

*Rod Stewart*

What people write about you is just not real.

*Van Morrison*

Interviews are stupid. It's so not reality. It's not conversation. Most of the time they want to talk about the album. I have absolutely nothing to say about it. It's an album, listen to it.

*J Mascis, Dinosaur Jr*

Reporter:  Who are your favorite performers? I don't mean folk, I mean general.

Bob Dylan: Rasputin . . . hmmm . . . Charles de Gaulle . . . the Staple Singers. I sort of have a general attitude about that. I like about everybody everybody else likes.

*Bob Dylan, from an early news conference*

Q. What's the difference between the old blues and the new?
A. Electricity.

*Jimi Hendrix, to Alan Goldman, critic*

Q: I hate to ask you this, but what comes first, the song or the words?
A: What comes first, the chicken or the egg?

*Donovan*

Q: How does it feel to be the Jesse James of rock?

A: William Bonney would be more accurate. Jesse James was motivated by greed, while Billy the Kid did it for the fun of it. All Americans are outlaws.

*Jim Morrison*

Q: Do you think of yourself primarily as a singer or a poet?

A: Oh, I think of myself more as a song and dance man, y'know.

*Bob Dylan, press conference at KQED*
*San Francisco, December 1965*

# there's good rockin' tonight!

People ask me, "Why do you wear makeup? Why don't you just come off the street?" The whole idea is you don't come off the street. You put on different clothes, you do your hair and you acquire this personality that has to go out and perform. When you get off the stage, that mask is dropped.

*Mick Jagger*

I thought rock 'n' roll dancing was disgusting. I wanted to be direct and real.

*David Byrne, on why he stood still*
*onstage while performing*

See, what they did was theatrics. We believe in entertainment. Just say what we are is "inner theater."

*Tommy Ramone, comparing David Bowie and*
*Rod Stewart to the Ramones*

My name is Edward Mahoney, and I'm working for this guy Eddie Money. I let him out of his cage for an hour and a half every night.

*Eddie Money*

It's just pure escapism. It's like going to see a film. People should just escape for a while, then they can go back to their problems. That's the way all songs should be: you listen to them, then discard them like a used tampon. I don't have any messages I'm trying to get across or anything.

*Freddie Mercury, on Queen's music*

I don't get to talk between songs very much; I'm always trying to get the songs going faster. So that's my way of bonding with the audience.

*Kurt Cobain, Nirvana, on diving from the stage during performances*

I like feedback. To me, feedback is a sound you can control, but you can never stop it. Feedback goes on forever. It's almost like surfing.

*Neil Young*

All performers, in my opinion, do not have the guts to do it alone in their room. They feel some need, and it might come from some deficiency in their life, some insecurity, some idiosyncrasy, something in their upbringing, which makes them feel the need to get up onstage, on a lighted platform, and tell everyone how they feel, and to be the center of attention for a little while.

*Henry Rollins*

Stage-diving doesn't bother me. It's just when there's one pair of boots that keeps getting someone in the head, that's a drag.

*Eddie Vedder, Pearl Jam*

Music is an hallucinogenic realm. When I'm singing and playing, I'm visiting another world. And when it gets really good, it's like there's a bright electric-blue white light that just radiates from everything and everybody. That's a place I go all the time. I like it there.

*Bob Weir, the Grateful Dead*

To play sober, to play straight, is like going to the dentist, I suppose. You're very, very nervous until the actual thing is taking place, then you call on some reserve inside you which is just waiting. Once you've got past the first couple of songs, you've broken the ice for yourself and for everyone else. I always relax after I've played my first solo.

*Eric Clapton*

The loudness of my vocal? That was a complete accident; it started because I used to sing Bob Dylan covers in pubs in Dublin, believe it or not. I used to get really annoyed when people would talk while I was singing so I used to just shout. I thought one day, "This sounds quite good."

*Sinead O'Connor*

If you know anything about energy, music is energy, and it's vibrations. The way it feels to me when I'm on the stage, especially when I'm having a really good show, I don't have to think about anything. All I'm doing is I'm not thinking, and it feels to me like a pure love with the audience. It's like a oneness, like rays of everybody's vibrations and energy level on your same one, and it's a weird feeling, it's love. It's sexual, it's not sexual . . . it's everything!

*Joan Jett*

Q: If you had to put into 25 words or less what it is you're
   trying to say when you get up on stage, what would it be?
A: LOOK AT ME!

*Joe Strummer, the Clash*

I was enchanted by the world of rock music—the way the singers could scream of good and evil, proclaim themselves angels or devils, and mortals would stand up and cheer. Sometimes they seemed the pure embodiment of madness.

*the Vampire Lestat, Anne Rice's fictional creation
from the novel of that name*

It's funny, but even within the space of one song, you can feel the audience come and go. The only thing to do is kick into a heavier gear and go for it. Some of our best gigs have been ones that start off badly and then become manic and unpredictable. Heavy but cool is the key.

*The Edge, U2*

You have to play on stage. That's the only way to learn. I never did it when I was young. Never seriously. You have to know how to deal with people, how to help them and let them help you as well. It's an interaction. And that comes from experience, I guess. I always find that when you're playing with other people, just listen and you'll know.

*Ry Cooder*

It feels really good to hold a note for days, to control the feedback on just one beam of power.

*Carlos Santana*

But you have to get out and play if you're going to be in music. Don't stay home and practice 'cos that's just like a boxer hittin' a heavy bag that don't hit back. You gotta have an audience.

*Ronnie Hawkins*

If a group just plays hit tunes, the audience tends to remember the tunes and not the group.

*Manfred Mann*

It's the greatest thing there is. . . . Some of the drudgery you have to go through on the road is so boring. . . . I wouldn't even care if there wasn't an audience there. It's just that you've got all the equipment set up, the musicians are there and paid for, the lights are on, it's just the right temperature, the stage is the right color, it's the right mood. And then you play, and you can create things right there.

*Frank Zappa, on playing live*

When the Dead are playing their best, blood drips from the ceiling in great, rich drops. Together we do a kind of suicide in music.

*Robert Hunter, lyricist for the Grateful Dead*

By playing live, you figure out what it is that makes people jump up and down and what it is that makes them sit in their chair.

*Chris Frantz, Talking Heads*

We all share the simultaneous experience of forgetting who we are at a rock concert, losing ourselves completely. When the music gets so good . . . everybody for a second forgets completely who they are and where they are. . . . If you have experienced that enough times, it starts to become something that you strive for, because it is so sweet.

*Pete Townshend*

I'm a worker, not a poser. My gowns aren't worn to be displayed. I work clothes. I'm not one who just likes to stand and sing. I can stand and sing in recording studios. Onstage, I need to perform.

*Tina Turner*

You know, it's a funny thing about music. The worst thing you can do is think. That's the lowest.

*Neil Young*

For me it was like I was an old car and I was being taken out for a ride at 100 miles an hour, and I kind of liked it because I was really getting rid of a lot of rust. I don't know if I'd like it night after night, and I'm not sure it isn't absolutely killing. You've got to be superhuman to play that stuff night after night and not have your senses wiped out by it.

*Norman Mailer, writer, on attending a Ramones show*

Howlin' Wolf, to me, was the greatest live act, because he did not have to move a finger when he performed. . . . I don't like people that jump around. When people think about Elvis moving around—he didn't jump around. He moved with grace . . . I love Mick Jagger. . . . But to see him jumping around like he does—I don't give a shit in what age, from Altamont to RFK Stadium—you don't have to do that, man. . . . Pushing rhythm and soul across. It's got nothin' to do with jumping around. I mean, what could it possibly have to do with jumping around?

*Bob Dylan*

Every time I go onstage I go back to that feeling of it being a primal fact of life and death whether my parents loved me or not. In order to get my parents' love at a certain point, I felt that it was necessary that I perform for them. Their love meant survival, so sometimes I transfer that to an audience, and if they don't love me, it's my death.

*Carly Simon*

Y'know, there's nothin' like tearing up a good club every now and then.

*Jerry Lee Lewis*

I feel like an actor when I'm onstage, rather than a rock artist. I very rarely have felt like a rock artist. I don't think that's much of a vocation, being a rock and roller.

*David Bowie*

I like it when people say, "I can't believe he wore that." We're in show business. The whole idea is to sleep late and wear cool clothes.

*Chris Isaak*

Every now and then I'll see people, but I basically see my mind, and I visualize and I see everybody and not really anybody. Because I put my heart and soul into it. Yeah.

*James Brown, on what he sees while performing*

# suicide right on the stage

What's it like? I would say it was a . . . powerful and pointed self-expression. There were a lot of reasons, not the least of which was that I didn't even know it was there at first.

*Iggy Pop, on rolling onstage in broken glass*

Because it was there. I was on two hits of orange sunshine, but actually I don't think I even had to be on stuff. I just like to smear things. Smearing is nice. Smearing is good.

*Iggy Pop, on smearing peanut butter*
*over his naked torso in performance*

You'll never see me rolling on the floor or crawling across a stage. It has something to do about grace.

*Eric Clapton*

# how to play, or: try carrying it around in a gunny sack

A painter starts with a blank canvas and as a musician, your canvas is silence. You don't want to cover it all up. So if you know what you're doing as a musician, you play the silences. You can't fall into that trap of trying to get everything in and playing so fast. If I want to travel fast, I'll take a sports car. You have to take time and pace yourself. Otherwise, technically you may make people go "wow," but it doesn't make good music.

*Keith Richards*

I just do everything the way I want to do it. Period. 'Cause that's the way it's easiest for me. Why make it hard on yourself? I mean, who is the God of Guitars who says it has to be held this way or that way? If in the end result you get the same noises and the same whatever, do it however you have to do it.

*Eddie Van Halen*

Essentially, the whole drumming thing is about getting as in shape as possible for that two hours. No sex, no wanking. It's the legs, mate. It's very important to stress that. Any drummer that has sex the night before he plays is being unprofessional. They tell a lot of athletes the same thing. Women weaken legs. My wife will love that.

*Pete Thomas, the Attractions*

It was obvious at the beginning that there were certain fundamentals that had to be observed. Coordinate with the bass drum, play the root of certain chords, and so forth. But after six months it was obvious to me that a lot of that could be disposed of.

*Phil Lesh, the Grateful Dead*

A lot of guitarists tend to throw their technique on you, which is a lot of crap, really. I've always thought that if you can clap your hands and stamp your feet in time, anyone can play guitar.

*Angus Young, AC/DC*

Part of the thing with rock guitar is that when you open an amplifier up, overtones come out; simple power chords, when played with volume, take up space in interesting ways; little things explode into big things.

*Danny Kortchmar, session musician*

My job in the band is to try to be the talking that goes on inside your brains, okay?

*Dave Thomas, Pere Ubu*

I didn't know anything about amplification, so I just got these amplifiers and tied bits of wire from one to another in this big, huge pile. It was a fantastic sound but it blew me up, so I decided to go and buy some real stuff.

*Jack Bruce*

When you steal from one guy it's plagerism, but if you steal from two or more it's research.

*Howard Roberts, studio musician*

The only chance I've got to be valid is to play from the heart, with soul.

*Joe Walsh*

Give me one note or a hundred, as long as you dredge up emotion.

*Billy Gibbons, ZZ Top*

There is kind of a code amongst most musicians, that if you're really satisfied with what you do, you must be dead, because you ain't growin'.

*Dr. John (Mac Rebennack)*

If you sing loud enough and hit drums hard enough everything's going to be all right.

*Don Dixon*

A good guitar riff is better than a solo. There are some like "The Last Time" by the Stones that are just one big riff.
*Sterling Morrison, the Velvet Underground*

I didn't ever see any reason to stop playing just because my fingers hurt. I was never impaired by the physical side of it. I thought it was something I had to do. It still goes for today.
*Ron Wood, the Rolling Stones*

I'm just a Skiffler, you know. I do "posh Skiffle." That's all it is.

*George Harrison*

And you know you don't have to have the intelligence of a brain surgeon to play rock and roll. The opposite is the general rule, in fact.

*Sting*

Reading music is like listening to flowers. I don't understand the concept.

*Paul Westerberg, the Replacements*

Even in the coffee houses folk musicians were divided into two camps: those who played Gibsons and those who played Martins. And the Gibson players played the blues and the Martin players preferred more melodic English and Irish ballads.

*Joni Mitchell*

I much prefer rhythm section playing, like when Jo Jones and Basie's All-American Rhythm Section were just floating along. What I mean is, I'm too worried about the time. If I actually had to count off a 32-bar solo, I'd die. I'd get to about 17 and lose count. I don't like the number game. It's necessary, and without it you have chaos. So you do need it, you know; but I don't like it. Having said all that, eighth- and quarter-notes are a load of crap, really. It's just a musical term for what is going *doing-doing*.

*Charlie Watts, the Rolling Stones*

There are times when I feel like the horn and I are one. But I haven't reached the ultimate communication yet. I'm still working toward it, I know it's there.

*Clarence Clemons*

It's called "Fake It 'Til You Make It." For the longest time, I pretended I was George Harrison, or Mick Jagger, or Keith Richards, or "Pinetop" Perkins when I played the piano. From the very beginning: "Jeez, I can sing a song better than that!" I was pretending. Kids do it. And I did it. And it worked.

*Steven Tyler, Aerosmith*

When I was young I was a real ugly duckling, too shy to even speak out loud in class, let alone get up on a stage. Up until the age of seventeen I was totally silent. I first started singing in the high school choir—that's the thing that allowed me to break the silence I had within myself.

*Ann Wilson, Heart*

It's easy to play like a machine and when a guy gets to playing like a machine, it's frightening. You've lost all feeling in it. We can appreciate how hard he practised and studied and probably skipped playing basketball and going with girls, but I still feel that in most cases, what is lacking is that the guy is not saying anything. And that's what music is all about. He can pick clean. But the music is expressionless.

*Les Paul*

It's about guitars. I once found a wonderful Fender stratocaster that quite obviously had been owned by Buddy Holly. You just played it and said, "Ahh!"

*Pete Townshend*

You get a first feeling that you're gonna be a drummer anywhere from six months to a year after you start. If you practice really hard you should have the feeling by then that you know what you're doing.

*Aynsley Dunbar, Jefferson Starship*

I learned a unique and indispensable skill, which is to make rock 'n' roll. I stopped my parents dressing me and started becoming a conniving cold-hearted son-of-a-bitch, which I've always been since the beginning of the Stooges.

*Iggy Pop*

With anything that you're doing, you reach a plateau and stay there for a while, and just through practice and familiarity something else happens.

*Tina Weymouth, Talking Heads*

I've been imitated so well I've heard people copy my mistakes.

*Jimi Hendrix*

# in the studio

Sonny, is it dumb enough?
*Phil Spector, to Sonny Bono in the studio, 1964*

To me, what's interesting is the indefinable. It's like recording. You meter everything that's going down on tape, and the lights are flashing, and you've got all these readings, but what you're looking to get on the record, there ain't a meter for. It's that feeling, that groove, that extra exhilaration, that lift, that air. And there's no meter in the world that can measure that. And that's what I look for, what I try to put in a record.
*Keith Richards*

What I do is almost all psychodynamics. You've gotta be indirect, create a diversion, trick the artist into giving something he doesn't wanna give. Something extra, magic—his soul, dammit. Good production borders on the criminal.
*Jim Dickinson, producer*

Actually, my big breakthrough as a producer was when I was producing "Watching the Detectives" and I discovered where the echo button was on the tape machine.
*Nick Lowe*

The idea for *Pet Sounds* was Brian's; it would be his favorite sounds, his pet sounds. He was fascinated by sounds and collecting them. He would experiment with tapes: we'd laugh in key and try different things just to see what we could do. It's that old thing of going maybe a little too far out to find what you can do, and then pulling back a bit to fit what you're actually doing.

*Carl Wilson, the Beach Boys*

When people ask me about recording and making music, I always say that the first rule is that there are no rules, and I wish more people would be aware of that. But if there was a rule it would be this: you can't shine shit.

*Nick Lowe*

Once I start playing, record whatever you get—I'm not gonna sit here and listen to quarter notes on a snare drum for five hours.

*Joe Walsh, on recording*

When we went to record, it I gave the words to Fred [Turner], but he said: "No way pal. It's your song, you sing it. Look at Dylan. You can sing, anyone can sing." So I sang.

*Randy Bachman, Bachman Turner Overdrive, on*
*"Takin' Care of Business"*

Everybody spent over $200,000 on theirs; mine was under $10,000. I think it's gotta cost under that to be a real rock 'n' roll record. I don't mind a few mistakes.

*Slim Dunlap, on recording his solo album compared with those of his ex Replacements bandmates*

---

# ike

I have slapped her. The times that I slapped her have mostly been about her looking sad.

*Ike Turner, on abusing Tina*

[Ike] saw himself as Phil Spector, as the driving force behind the star. I saw him as the driving force behind a lot of things. It was the first time I saw a guy pistol-whip another guy in his own band. Ike acted like a goddamned pimp.

*Keith Richards*

# cult status

You can only be a cult band so long. I'm thirty-two years old. I don't want to be a cult fucking hero. We went through that, and it's great and it's flattering, but those people should go out into their clubs and find the next new band. That's what alternative music is all about. It's like "You were right that time. See if you can do it again."

*Bill Berry, R.E.M.*

Every time we've put out a record, someone has accused us of selling out. There are people who don't really want a band they like to get too big. . . . Being from New York, people have this idea you should stay arty or whatever.

*Kim Gordon, Sonic Youth*

People often ask me what the difference is between being indie and on a major label; it's cell phones, I fucking hate those things.

*Mark Eitzel, American Music Club*

When I think back to the days at the Marquee—we got a regular Tuesday night residency, which was a big coup for us because we didn't even have a record out. The first night, there were maybe fifty people, the next night, two hundred, and after that we were packing it. We were a cult within a cult—our whole audience was nineteen years old, as we were—and there's a great feeling of affirmation when the audience knows they're sharing in the success; they're making the success happen as well. So you become incredibly close. The two or three thousand people who regularly attended the Marquee residency—I think I know them all by their first names.

*Pete Townshend*

As far as we're concerned, signing to a major has gotten us to the point where if someone comes to see us play, they can go buy our records. We want that. And we don't make any bones about that; we want to participate in our culture. We don't go without seeing our moms for a year so we can be cool. We do it because we want to play music and be a part of people's lives.

*Billy Corgan, Smashing Pumpkins*

Look, anyone who performs in the recording industry and on most stages is already in the realm of commercial music. So there's no differentiation except in terms of the number of people your audience is comprised of. How far and to what extent does your music reach the people?

*Ross Valory, Journey*

With the [Sex] Pistols, we were hated, absolutely despised. There was no audience there at all to any great extent. We sold a few records in a small banana republic called Britain.

They never changed the world really until we became defunct and ceased to exist. Now it's seen in quite a different light. And that's not fair.

*John Lydon*

A lot of people who are listening to so-called underground music have become intolerant. The whole thing started as a plea for tolerance, but now it's come full circle. People have become almost fascist, they've become very intolerant of anything that's not their musical scene.

*John Peel, BBC music host, 1970*

# guitar smashing 101

I smash guitars because I like them.

*Pete Townshend*

When Pete smashed his guitar it was because 'e was pissed off. . . . When I smashed me drums, it was because I was pissed off. We were frustrated. You're working as hard as you can to get that fucking song across, to get that audience by the balls, to make it an event. When you've done all that, when you've worked your balls off and you've given the audience everything you can give, and they don't give anything back, that's when the fucking instruments go, because: "You fucking bastards! We've worked our fucking balls off! And you've given us nothing back!"

*Keith Moon*

One night I banged the guitar on the ceiling. It was fantastic visually, with my legs spread and everything. In the second set I banged it on the ceiling again and it broke. There were a few laughs, mainly negative reaction. So I carried on and smashed it to bits. It gave me a fantastic buzz. The audience really liked it and I started to do it as part of the act. Now it has become a rather artificial finish. . . . We want to get out of car accidents and into music.

> Pete Townshend, on the origin of
> smashing his guitar, 1968

I used to break guitars a lot more. Most of the destruction was because we were frustrated—our equipment didn't work very often. Now that it works, I don't do it as much.

> Kurt Cobain, Nirvana

Antonioni was an awkward bastard. . . . So he says to me [adopts Italian accent], "We want you to break your guitar." I said, "Oh yeah, a 1954 Les Paul and you want me to smash it? Get away." He said, "Don't be ridiculous, we pay for it." I said, "You can't replace that." So then they got Hofner to bring down these shitty guitars. So I had this tea-chest full of these £25 joke guitars. Those guitars were just destined to be smashed and I went right through 'em three or four at a time with this Hofner rep standing watching at the side. He thought it was all great fun.

> Jeff Beck, on the filming of Michelangelo
> Antonioni's Blow Up

It's powerful when Kurt [Cobain] does it or Pete Townshend. Maybe not so powerful when Garth Brooks does it. Garth shouldn't be smashing guitars in my humble opinion. He just doesn't get it. He's just not a smasher.

*John Hiatt*

I encourage them because they always have to go out and buy more guitars.

*Les Paul*

# riot GRRRLS!!!

We were starting to see these articles people were writing
about us, and you could feel the hatred. They wanted to
know why girls were playing rock 'n' roll, and do you think
the fact that you got female skin makes the strings sound
different. Different than what? I mean, I'm telling you, people were really askin' us these questions.

*Joan Jett*

Women are going to be the new Elvises. That's the only place
for rock 'n' roll to go. The only people who can express anything new in rock are girls, and gays.

*Deborah Harry, 1981*

I'd say just recently, within the past six months or so, people
will come up to me and, instead of saying, "You're a good
drummer for a girl," they'll say, "Hey, you're a pretty good
drummer." So that's kind of neat. But if they say, "You're a
good drummer for a girl," that's cool, too. If they like it,
that's all that counts, really.

*Gina Schock, the Go-Go's, 1982*

I think it's fun that people like the band because we're girls.
I mean, we write about being girls and we look like girls and
we live life as girls and—we are girls. I don't really give a

damn if people think it's different . . . well, we are a little different.

*Susanna Hoffs, the Bangles*

People still distinguish the Graces as an all-female band. They don't say U2 is an all-male band.

*Charlotte Caffey, ex Go-Go's, on her new band*

What if a little girl picked up a guitar and said "I wanna be a rock star." Nine times out of ten her parents would never allow her to do it. We don't have so many lead guitar women, not because women don't have the ability to play the instrument but because they're kept locked up, taught to be something else. I don't appreciate that.

*David Lee Roth*

# turn it up!

Too loud. The country may be producing a new generation of young Americans with impaired hearing before they are 21.

*Ralph Nader, on highly amplified rock*

A: I have this thing every night when I go to bed. I have to leave the TV up really loud because my head's ringing so bad. It goes, "zzzzzzzzzzzzz." If I turn the TV up, I don't hear it as much.

Q: How long has this TV thing been going on?

A: Uh, since, like, '82. I'm starting to get a little worried.

*Bob Mould, Sugar, 1992*

They're trying to mesmerize you, not let you hear the music.

*Tom Lyons, road manager of the Cowsills,*
*on "hard rock groups"*

I like listening to the loud music. Of course, a lot of pop groups use the excessive sound to cover their mistakes. That's the approach of hard rock. Also, some of them believe that the music is more important than the lyrics.

*Paul Cowsill, the Cowsills*

I play when I can but it wasn't until recenly that I have been able to practice without bothering people. When I lived in San Francisco I couldn't play loud, but now I have my own house and I can play anything I want.

*Steve Miller*

It was so loud. It was, like, 130 decibels. That's very unhealthy, but the idea is to just tear people's heads off and hand 'em back as they leave.

*Bob Mould, Sugar, on the band's debut show*
*at which record company staffers distributed*
*earplugs to the audience*

Even though my hearing seems to have declined, I can still perceive things, although they tend to be loud, the things that I perceive.

*Phil Lesh, the Grateful Dead*

If the kids can hear the words, they'll turn their radio down. We want them to turn it up. It sort of relieves a kid's anxieties if he can drown out his parents.

*Jan Berry, Jan and Dean, 1965*

# #1 with a bullet

People change when they get a hit. Your back straightens.
Your acne goes. I know, because it happened to me.

*Peter Noone, Herman's Hermits*

I'd like to have a hit record because Little Richard had 'em,
Buddy Holly had 'em, and Bob Dylan had 'em. I know this
sounds highfalutin' and all that, but you can't affect culture
without getting a hit record on the radio.

*Dave Alvin, the Blasters*

I think it's great I have a hit single. People say to me, "Do you
think you sold out?" They should be saying, "Oh, wow,
you're on AM radio."

*Patti Smith*

No, it was, "Why write a song about a state?" And "Monday
Monday"—"A song about a day of the week? Big deal!" "Go
Where You Wanna Go"—"Who cares where you go?" I got
all these answers.

*John Phillips, the Mamas and the Papas, on initial
reactions to "California Dreamin' " and other hits*

I remember Mick Jagger's jaw dropping the first time he saw
us. He couldn't believe that four such uncool people, at that

time, could have a bigger hit than he did. The Kinks were seriously rebellious and threatening, because we knew no shame.

*Ray Davies, the Kinks*

People always ask why we're still together. [It's] because we don't have a hit single and we still gotta work for a living.
*Dee Dee Ramone, the Ramones, on the band's fifteenth anniversary in 1989; he quit the band weeks later*

To have a huge hit record with only three chords is one of the best tricks a writer can do.

*Burton Cummings, the Guess Who*

I just concentrate on one hit at a time.

*Phil Spector*

# what a drag it is getting old

My music is like water. And is there such a thing as adult water and kid water? I wanna know. The common denominator is life.

*James Brown*

When I'm 33, I'll quit. That's the time when a man has to do something else. I can't say what it will definitely be. It's still in the back of my head—but it won't be in show business. I don't want to be a rock star all my life. I couldn't bear to end up as an Elvis Presley and sing in Las Vegas with all those housewives and old ladies coming in with their handbags. It's really sick.

*Mick Jagger, 1972*

Since no one else does what we do, let's see where we can go with it. After all, there really isn't a chronological point where you aren't allowed to rock anymore.

*Joe Perry, Aerosmith*

I foresee standing at a microphone with an orchestra of rock musicians, not classical. They could play my music as recorded. I could stand and sing, maybe dance a little, but not the stuff I'm doing now. I'm smarter than that. I would be embarrassed. When I start to shrink, I'm going to find another way.

*Tina Turner*

## hope i die before i get old

The funny thing about that, which I realized the other day, is that if I went back to the time when I said that and knew that I hadn't died before I became old, I think I would have been fucking angry. In a sense I've betrayed myself in that respect. But perhaps if I had died before I got old, I might have been forgotten. You tend to hope you'll become James Dean or Jimi Hendrix, but a lot of dead people aren't remembered at all. So I haven't been able to achieve that one great ambition I had when I was nineteen. But I've tried to compensate by actually making myself happy.

*Pete Townshend, on "My Generation"*

You get to a certain age and you start to enshrine whatever it was that was great when you were youngest and happiest. It happens to me a lot. If you hear something new that everybody else likes you get defensive. "That's not like the Kinks' 'You Really Got Me.' It's got no melody like 'Ruby Tuesday.'" It's a trap but I go through it, too. I try consciously not to do it.

*Iggy Pop*

The teeny bopper age is not over. There have been teeny bopper singers and groups for years now and I think that there always will be. Probably half the hippies on the scene now were teeny boppers a couple of years ago. It's all a question of age.

*Ray Dorey, Edison Lighthouse, 1970*

I've never been worried about my age, per se, because every time I write a song, every time we make a record, every time I walk on stage, I'm every bit as scared as I was when I started. I'm still constantly between despair and elation, and that's a big part of what keeps me going.

*Ray Davies, the Kinks*

I think that leaping around on a rock and roll stage, acting like you're 25 when you're 50, is idiotic. I find it sort of sad when old singers try to act young. It's pathetic rather than interesting.

*Grace Slick*

**175**

In art or theater or literature, nobody says, "I'm sorry, pal, you're 45, you've got to spend the rest of your life reading the same book or seeing the same film or going to the same play."

*John Peel, BBC DJ, on keeping up with new music*

You don't even know what you're doing until about 45. And I don't think—as a musician—you really hit your peak until you're about 60. Let me go out like Dizzy Gillespie. Let me be around and play.

*Steve Miller*

Obviously, if you get to a point where you're doddering around the stage and you can't fuckin' move without falling down and breaking your hip, then it's time to call it a day.

*Joe Perry, Aerosmith*

When I went to see John Lee Hooker for the first time when I was, like, 17—I thought, he's so old. He'll never be able to carry on much longer. And he must have been about 38 then. And he's still there. Either you're dead or you move along.

*Mick Jagger*

# it's better to burn out than to fade away

I hate it. It's better to fade away like an old soldier than to burn out. I don't appreciate worship of dead Sid Vicious or of dead James Dean or of dead John Wayne. It's the same thing. Making Sid Vicious a hero, Jim Morrison—it's garbage to me. I worship the people who survive. Gloria Swanson, Greta Garbo. . . . I don't want Sean worshipping . . . Sid Vicious. What do they teach you? Nothing. Death. Sid Vicious died for what? So that we might rock? I mean, it's garbage, you know. If Neil Young admires that sentiment so much, why doesn't he do it? Because he sure as hell faded away and came back many times, like all of us. No, thank you. I'll take the living and the healthy.

*John Lennon, 1980*

The rock 'n' roll spirit is not survival. Of course the people who play rock 'n' roll should survive. But the essence of the rock 'n' roll spirit, to me, is that it's better to burn out really bright than it is to sort of decay off into infinity. Even though if you look at it in a mature way, you'll think, "Well, yes . . . you should decay off into infinity, and keep going along." Rock 'n' roll doesn't look that far ahead. Rock 'n' roll is right now. What's happening right this second. Is it bright? Or is it dim because it's waiting for tomorrow—that's what people want to know. And that's why I say that.

*Neil Young, asked to respond to Lennon's*
*comments two years later*

# everybody's sayin' music is love

I believe in the folk ethic. I believe that's what music is all about: music for people, by people. It's Woody Guthrie and it's punk rock, and I'm trying to bridge that gap. Because that's my lifetime. I started out with punk rock, and I discovered Woody Guthrie, and I realized it was all the same thing. It was an important revelation to me.

*Dave Pirner, Soul Asylum*

Part of music's primary function has always been to get people to celebrate or to produce changes of consciousness. That's what music is about. It changes your mood; it produces the heroic background music for your own life.

*Jerry Garcia*

Music's a book that's, like, too big to read, so it's O.K. to study it, 'cause I'd never get through it anyway.

*Eric Schenkman, the Spin Doctors*

A lot of musicians look to music to either release tension or avoid it, and it's a huge defocusing element.

*David Navarro, ex Jane's Addiction*

I've always said that hard rock, or big rock music, the kind of music we play, is simply folk music delivered at high velocity. Shot from guns. We simply reflect what we see in newspapers, magazines, what you've lived and breathed before.

*David Lee Roth*

Music has tremendous value to me, but it's a very subjective thing. It's like religion in a way. As soon as you start talking about it, it just goes like a flat pancake. And then it's rubbish. We're back to Spinal Tap again.

*Annie Lennox*

Sex and music are still for me places where you glimpse God. Sex and art, I suppose, but unless you're going to get slain in the spirit by a Warhol or Rothko, I think for most of us art is music.

*Bono*

I think you plug into this electricity. It's like a river in a way; no question. When the magic's there, everyone in the room feels it. You're a bit like a radio aerial and you quiver when you're on to something.

*Peter Gabriel, on creativity*

I think the function of art is to reflect God and to try to remember all the knowledge that we had before we were born, of how powerful we are and what God is. I think that's the drive to create, to fill the space, to fill the emptiness, even for just two seconds, so as to achieve the sense of having reflected, of having opened up and connected, with whatever it is that is above us.

*Sinead O'Connor*

Music does my wishing for me.

*Exene Cervenka*

We didn't do it exactly like the older fellows—just with no beat to it. We put the beat with it. Put a little drive to it. . . . We went to putting time to our low down Mississippi Blues. We put a pretty good group together because we learned the beat, we learned what the people's moving off of. Even if it's the blues, we still had to drive behind it.

*Muddy Waters*

I played with a lot of West Indians, Puerto Ricans, Jamaicans, Spanish boys, Hungarians. I just copied all their changes and beats and the ones I liked, I kept 'em.

*Professor Longhair (Henry Roeland Byrd)*

Music is what you do because you can't speak.

*PJ Harvey*

Music can save people, but it can't in the commercial way it's being used. It's just too much. It's pollution. Have you ever been in the city, walking down the street, and the car comes down the street, "Boom, boom, boom, boom, boom." It's like a "Jaws" movie or something. It's frightening. You know it is. "Boom, boom, boom, boom, boom." You want to take a machine gun and blast it off the street.

*Bob Dylan*


Well, I started playing music around '73. I'd tried everything else, and I couldn't find anything I wanted to do or anywhere to be. So I got into music because it seemed like the best thing around. You could say it was the thing that had the least laws and restrictions about it.

*Joe Strummer, the Clash, 1981*


I think it's a question of heritage. European musicians tend to come from a classical heritage. American bands tend to come from a blues-based heritage. It's not true in all cases, but it tends to be. There lie your fundamental differences between bands like ELP, Yes and The Moody Blues, and bands like the Allman Brothers.

*Greg Lake, Emerson, Lake and Palmer,*
*on ELP's classical approach to music*


Rap is like the polio vaccine. At first no one believed in it. Then, once they knew it worked, everyone wanted it.

*Grandmaster Flash, 1991*


Funk is its own reward.

*George Clinton*

# what's that sound?

It's the territory, and the river, and the three states and all that. It's roots. There would have been a "Memphis sound" anyway—if it hadn't been us, it would have been somebody else.

*Steve Cropper, Booker T. and the MGs*

Maybe it's the river. Because it goes from New Orleans to St. Louis. And Chicago's a part of it too. . . . Maybe it sounds crazy, but maybe that river has something to do with that much music coming from there. There's no other river in the world that feels like it when you look at it, when you get close to it.

*Booker T., Booker T. and the MGs, on*
*American music associated with the*
*Memphis–Northern Mississippi Delta*

Well, I can relate to "down home," you know. Musicians who come up in the South, musicians who come up on the West Coast, the East Coast, anywhere. That environment affects their heads. In most cities you have a whole bunch of other static going on. Down South, living in a small town, Macon, you have a lot of time to put into it. You have a lot of time to check out other stuff, to check out a lot of stuff in your head.

*Lamar Williams, the Allman Brothers Band,*
*on "Southern Blues"*

I call it secular gospel music.

*Daryl Hall, on "Philadelphia Soul"*

I'm not exactly sure what the "Motown Sound" is, but when Moe gets back to town I'm going to find out what it's all about.

*Jimmy Durante, on "The Hollywood Palace"*
*television show*

I like music that's quirky and eclectic. That's what I'm interested in.

*Sting*

To me music is not notes played perfectly, it's the right rhythm. I don't believe in A-D-E or any of that, and contrary to popular belief, you cannot dance to rock 'n' roll. Everything, bass, drums and guitar plays the same tune, the louder and more distorted the better, until it becomes a wash whose sole purpose is to induce stupidity.

*John Lydon*

My music is for an escape. I just want to make all these people feel good. That's what the great thing is for me: that love, that contact, that pure rock 'n' roll moment.

*Joan Jett*

I like it best when I hear it coming through the wall in a hotel room. I like it best on a bad speaker from a block away.

*Tom Waits, on listening to music*


I like music you can tell is human made.

*Steve Turner, Mudhoney*


In our music we're looking for the big enema, the big catharsis.

*Gerald Casale, Devo*


Trash is more party than thought. It's dumb. Somebody's always gonna buy trash. Maybe not everybody, but somebody. As long as you write good trash, you're gonna do all right. I think music's getting simpler. I hope so. A lot of new wave is too intellectual.

*Joe "King" Carrasco, 1980*


Music's gotten so serious these days. MTV is so profound, so suicidal. We've only got 50 or 60 years here, and I'm not about to spend it all with a cross hanging over my back. Lighten up. It's just rock and roll. Fats Domino singing "Blueberry Hill"—that's the apex of rock and roll. That's what it's all about.

*Chris Goss, Masters of Reality*


I'm against puttin' all names on music. It just causes more confusion. Like you can say "voodoo rock" . . . but it's all music. What I play is music. What everybody plays is music. If it's symphonic or it's jazz, it's still music. It don't make no difference if it's hillbilly or rock and roll or what, because it's still music. If you like it, it's good. If you don't like it, it's bad. It's bad to you.

*Dr. John (Mac Rebennack)*

Music should sound the way it did on my high school car radio.

*Don Fleming, Gumball*

The fact of the matter is, everybody I know is second string to music for me. I cannot explain to anybody, including the closest people in my life, how music is more important than all of them.

*Dave Pirner, Soul Asylum*

# the new secular religion

But for some reason I seem to be a performer. And something extraordinary does happen, this invisible bridge between a performer and an audience. At its worst it's diabolical, at its best it's amazing and almost essential. We don't have a church, the West has lost its faith, so we've got to have some space where we can lose ourselves and experience something that isn't everyday. But the fear is that you could become Spinal Tap.

*Annie Lennox*

We use volume to drive the evil spirits out the back of your head, and by evil spirits I mean the job, the boss, the spouse, the probation officer. Hopefully when you walk out of our show you'll feel like the building could fall on you and nothing would happen. People do leave our shows feeling that way and it's the same feeling other people go to church or hockey games for.

*David Lee Roth, Van Halen, 1981*

What we play is "trance-dance music," music that creates a liberating, getting-out-of-yourself trance that transcends the ordinary. People use pop music today in the same way as they used to use religious music—to achieve states of ecstasy. It's like what Joseph Campbell said about the old myths not applying anymore. Pop music provides the new myths and hence the new spirituality.

*Kate Pierson, the B-52's*

God is man-made. We invented this to keep other members of mankind and especially womankind under control. It's a protectionist racket. Humans can't live without magic— gods, pop stars, clowns, UFOs.

*Andy Partridge, XTC*

Music is incredibly effective. Performers are the priests of our time—they can draw attention to moral issues.

*Larry Cox, of Amnesty International, on rock benefits*

To me it's a religion. For instance, I can feel just blah, but when I get on that stage, there'll be so much energy flowing from the other five cats that they just lift me in a real strong spiritual way, 'til I don't know how tired I am. It becomes a real strong spiritual thing to get to the point where the six cats on that stage, their job is to produce a sound, the Allman sound. But I don't think it can be put in any particular category.

*Lamar Williams, the Allman Brothers Band*

# personal
# observations

Elvis killed himself over a broad. It took five of them to put me in the shape I'm in today.

*Jerry Lee Lewis*

He had the kind of music that no one else was doing. He would sit down with a guitar and start playing and making up stuff, different every time, it just kept coming out, coming out, coming out. . . . Then he would stop and you would never hear that one again. Musically, I thought he was very unique.

*Neil Young, on Charles Manson*

Of course, I made numerous mistakes, too. I was a bit of a flake at the time. But I never felt dogmatic about inflicting pain as a way of life, you know? Not like some groups coming along now. I never called myself "Iggy Crush" or "Iggy Squeeze-Vomit." It was always just Iggy Pop, just a part of what was goin' on. There's not a total commitment to tragedy here.

*Iggy Pop*

I've always wanted to be Brigitte Bardot.

*Bob Dylan, 1966*

I know it has a certain amount of baggage because it's played by rich people with terrible taste in trousers who are racist snobs, and I'm sorry about that. But golf is very meditational.

*Mike Mills, R.E.M.*

A lot of artists are aliens. They're really a bunch of geeks when you get right down to it.

*Walter Becker, Steely Dan*

And I'd like to meet Madonna! I'd say, "Gee, you're pretty!" I seriously doubt she's a virgin but that's a good song.

*Brian Wilson, the Beach Boys*

I would never consider myself a musician; I'm just an entertainer.

*Johnny Thunders, the New York Dolls*

Mainly, I helped wipe out the sixties.

*Iggy Pop*

I was the king of cock-rock, and I still am on a good night.

*Robert Plant, Led Zeppelin*

There's a point where you find yourself tiptoeing as an artist, and then you know that you're in the wrong place. It's like you have a rule book, but you don't remember where you got it.

*Bono*

If I'm a guitar hero, I never entered the competition—I forgot to fill in the application form.

*Keith Richards*

but rhythms like rules shift.

*Patti Smith*

Personally, I get a good feeling when people take their hard-earned money and spend it on something I'm involved with. It makes me feel that we're doing something valid. I don't believe in subsidized art.

*Wendy O. Williams, the Plasmatics*

Rick did something that was probably every kid's dream, to pick up a guitar and rock the kids at the party.

*Erik Anderson, singer/songwriter, on Rick Nelson*

I have the amount of cars I do because I smash them up a lot. Six are always in the garage; it's fact. They're always saying I'm a capitalist pig. I suppose I am. But, ah . . . it ah . . . it's good for me drumming, I think. OH-HOOOOO-HA-HAHA!

*Keith Moon*

If everyone uses them there won't be any more me or Jimi Hendrix or anyone like that. If you take it that far, you can buy a computer that will play all the music you want. Press a button and it will improvise for hours on end.

*Eric Clapton, on synthesizers, 1967*

Once you get in trouble with the police, you're always in trouble and that's it.

*Mick Jagger, 1968*

Yeah, well my daddy he didn't leave me too much. You know he was a very simple man, but what he told me was this: he did say, "Son," . . . he said so many things, you know? He said, "Son, it's possible to become so defiled in this world that your own mother and father will abandon you. And if this happens, God will always believe in your own ability to mend your ways."

*Bob Dylan, accepting a Grammy award, 1991*

It was just about what was going on. You know, the punky attitude that had to do with music—hate your mother and stab your father. It's kind of a trend of some sort, and this was a statement that we weren't there. We don't hate our mothers and fathers.

*Robbie Robertson, on including a photo of the Band's relatives in the* Big Pink *album*

I'm not really here, I just stick around for my friends.

*Captain Beefheart*


There are plenty of rules left just waiting to be broken and I'll do my part.

*Laurie Anderson*


More than anything, I wanted to be Hank Williams. I even stayed drunk for three years once trying to be like him. It didn't work.

*T-Bone Burnette*


I feel that Byrds albums are electronic magazines. We have special issues like on country. We have cartoons, editorials and political opinions. I like the term electronic magazine. I like the term electronics, I like electronics.

*Roger McGuinn, the Byrds*


What movie stars used to have in the way of public appeal, the rock and roll bands have taken over. It isn't so much what the rock and roll musicians are doing, it's what the kids are doing with the pop musicians. The larger than life thing. It's like John Lennon is much more important than Vanessa Redgrave; whereas Paul Whiteman was never more important than Gary Cooper.

*Stephen Stills, 1970*

It's like, we musicians have a responsibility to turn people on to their spiritual awareness, not just please their meat level.

*Dr. John (Mac Rebennack)*

Lack of irony is not exactly my specialty.

*Donald Fagen*

You must, after the age of 33, continue to do a certain type of work, or else go into the shoe business; forget music or it'll turn into hatred, or else reiteration, redundance and in many cases death.

*Garth Hudson, the Band*

Our best jobs were fraternity parties. The only real problem we'd run into there was that every now and then they'd set fire to our equipment. Other than that fraternity brothers made for a very easy going audience. What ever song they requested, we'd play "Land of 1,000 Dances" and they'd be happy. They were too busy throwing up on their dates to notice. They are running the nation today.

*Dave Barry, humorist, on his life and times*
*as a "guitar slinger"*

We long for a way out but lack the right moves, verbs and curves. So we lift a hair, a gesture, a way of dress. Any means necessary to break out. . . .

We go through life. We shed our skins. We become ourselves. Ultimately we are not seeking others to bow to, but to reinforce our individual natures, to help us suffer our own choices, to guide us on our own particular journeys.

*Patti Smith, on finding heroes and heroines*

I had to come to you behind the Rolling Stones and Beatles.

*Muddy Waters, to an audience at Stanford University, 1967*

At this age I think I learned that some things are supposed to be easy and some things are supposed to be hard. And maybe what I'd done in the past was make the hard things easy and the easy things hard.

*Warren Zevon*

Look, we're all maladjusted little weirdos or we wouldn't be doing this.

*Don Henley*

If it all ended tomorrow, we'd be rich and out of work.

*John Lennon, on the future of the Beatles, 1964*

I'd get up in the morning and maybe some guy is trying to weasel me into some sneaky deal and somebody else is trying to cheat me out of something but my kitty just wants to roll around and play. I go into kitty world and completely forget the other shit. It's great.

*Iggy Pop, on how cat ownership changed his life*

Q: What was your favorite show as a kid?

A: *Shindig,* the '60s rock-and-roll show. In fact, during my favorite musical moments on *Letterman*—when I'm playing with James Brown, Steve Winwood, or Booker T. and the MGs—in my mind, I'm really performing on *Shindig.*

*Paul Shaffer, CBS Orchestra*


I compare the twist to the electric light. The twist is dancing *apart* to popular music, and before Chubby Checker, that did not exist. The twist is me, and I'm it. I *am* the electric light.

*Chubby Checker*


I took up music so I wouldn't have to talk to people.

*Richard Thompson*


I used to spend the summers up there [Nashville], just to get away from Florida for a while, you know. I'd go visit my grandma. And this kid named John Banion lived across the street and he had an old Silvertone guitar. John taught me a couple of chords on it and stuff, and I got kinda interested in it, and my brother Gregg did, too. In fact, Gregg learned to play first, and I kinda lost interest in it, man.

*Duane Allman, the Allman Brothers Band*

# a w w   m o m !!!

Having your parents' blessing is so important. May-be not on the surface, but deep down.

*Joan Jett*

My parents still don't understand what I do, really. My dad thinks that I've been fired from my job for the past two years, because I haven't been onstage. God.

*Paul Westerberg, the Replacements*

# my first gig

I remember it was the night of the junior prom, and I was playing a roadhouse, performing Neil Diamond songs. We were paid in amphetamines. It was the start of a great career, believe me.

*Paul Westerberg, the Replacements*

The first time I ever did it we had these Beatle jackets on, and we looked cool and this girl I had a crush on was staring at me, and at the end of the night the priest gave me 15 bucks. I never had a second thought; from then on I always just loved the gig.

*Billy Joel*

# sources

## newspapers and magazines:

Aquarian Weekly
The Baltimore Sun
Bazaar
College Papers
Crawdaddy
The Daily Dope
Details
Downbeat
Elle
Entertainment Weekly
Esquire
Feature
Guitar Player
Guitar World
Interview
The Los Angeles Times
Melody Maker
Mondo 2000
Music Scene
Musician
New Musical Express
Newsweek
New York
The New York Post
The New York Times
Off Beat
Oui
Paper
Penthouse
People
The Philadelphia Inquirer

*Playboy*
*Pulse!*
*Q*
*Reality Hackers*
*The Record*
*Rock Compact Disc*
*Rock Magazine*
*Rock & Roll Confidential*
*Rolling Stone*
*Spin*
*Time*
*Trouser Press*
*TV Guide*
*Us*
*USA Today*
*Utne Reader*
*Vanity Fair*
*Variety*
*The Village Voice*
*Vogue*
*Voice Rock & Roll Quarterly*
*The Washington Times*
*The Washington Post*
*Wet*

## books:

*No Matter How You Slice It, It's Still Baloney,* Jean Arbeiter, Quill Press, 1984

*Route 666: On the Road to Nirvana,* Gina Arnold, St. Martin's Press, 1993

*Dave Barry's Greatest Hits,* Dave Barry, Fawcett, 1988

*Teenage Idol, Travelin' Man,* Philip Bashe, Hyperion, 1992

*The Ramones: An American Band,* Jim Bessman, St. Martin's Press, 1993

*Hal Blaine & the Wrecking Crew,* Hal Blaine/David Goggin, Mix Books, 1990

*Keith Richards: The Biography,* Victor Bockris, Poseidon Press/ Simon & Schuster, 1992

*The Rolling Stones Chronicle,* Massimo Bonanno, Henry Holt, 1990

*Rhythm Oil,* Stanley Booth, Pantheon, 1991

*Musicians in Tune,* Jenny Boyd, Fireside, 1992

*Inside Pop 2,* David Dachs, Scholastic Book Services, 1970

*Rolling Stones in Their Own Words,* David Dalton and Mick Farren, Quick Fox, 1980

*Rock Names,* Adam Dolgins, Citadel Press, 1993

*The Age of Rock,* Jonathan Eisen, Vintage, 1969

*The Age of Rock 2,* Jonathan Eisen, Vintage, 1970

*Good Rockin' Tonight,* Colin Escott/Martin Hawkins, St. Martin's Press, 1991

*On the Road with the Rolling Stones,* Chet Flippo, Doubleday/Dolphin, 1985

*Hickory Wind,* Ben Fong-Torres, Pocket Books, 1991

*The Rolling Stone Rock 'n' Roll Reader,* Ben Fong-Torres, Bantam, 1974

*What's That Sound?,* Ben Fong-Torres, Anchor Press/Doubleday, 1976

*Sound Effects,* Simon Frith, Pantheon Books, 1982

*She's a Rebel,* Gillian G. Gaar, Seal Press, 1992

*Conversations with the Dead,* David Gans, Citadel Press, 1991

*Bill Graham Presents,* Bill Graham/Robert Greenfield, Doubleday, 1992

*One Is the Loneliest Number,* Jimmy Greenspoon/Mark Bego, Pharos Books, 1991

*Grateful Dead: The Official Book of the Deadheads,* Paul Grushkin (ed.), Quill, 1983

*Rock: A World Bold as Love,* Douglas Hall and Sue C. Clark, Cowles, 1970

*Rock 'n' Roll Babylon,* Gary Herman, Perigee, 1982

*From the Velvets to the Voidoids,* Clinton Heylin, Penguin, 1993

*The Penguin Book of Rock & Roll Writing,* Clinton Heylin (ed.), Penguin, 1992

*Laurie Anderson,* John Howell, Thunder's Mouth Press, 1992

*Across the Great Divide,* Barney Huskyns, Hyperion, 1993

*The Lizard King: The Essential Jim Morrison,* Jerry Hopkins, Scribners, 1992

*They Made a Monkee Out of Me,* Davy Jones, Dome Press, 1987

*Love, Janis,* Laura Joplin, Villard Books, 1992

*Rock Folk,* Michael Lydon, Citadel Press, 1990

*The First Rock & Roll Confidential Report,* Dave Marsh, Pantheon, 1985

*The Book of Rock Lists,* Dave Marsh and Kevin Stein, Dell/Rolling Stone Press, 1984

*The Aesthetics of Rock,* R. Meltzer, Something Else Press, Inc., 1970

*Secrets from the Masters,* Don Menn, GPI Books, 1992

*Stairway to Heaven,* Tom Miller/Jim Hornfischer, HarperCollins, 1992

*Sex, Art and American Culture,* Camille Paglia, Vintage Books, 1992

*Scandal Annual 1992,* The Paragon Project, St. Martin's Press, 1991

*Scandal Annual 1991,* The Paragon Project, St. Martin's Press, 1990

*The Triumph of Vulgarity: Rock Music in the Mirror of Romanticism,* Robert Pattison, Oxford University Press, 1987

*Totally Uninhibited,* Lawrence J. Quark, Quill, 1991

*The Vampire Lestat,* Anne Rice, Alfred A. Knopf, 1985

*The Rolling Stone Interviews 1967–1980,* The Editors of Rolling Stone, St. Martin's Press/Rolling Stone Press, 1981

*The Rolling Stone Interviews,* The Editors of Rolling Stone, Straight Arrow/Paperback Library, 1971

*England's Dreaming,* Jon Savage, St. Martin's Press, 1992

*Monterey Pop,* Joel Selvin, Chronicle Books, 1992

*Saucerful of Secrets,* Nicholas Shaffner, Delta, 1991

*The Rockin' 50s,* Arnold Shaw, DaCapo Books, 1974

*Simpson's Contemporary Quotations,* James B. Simpson, Houghton Mifflin Co., 1988

*Break It Down,* Michael Small, Citadel Press, 1992

*Rock 'n' Roll Confidential,* Penny Stallings, Little, Brown, 1984

*The Cure: A Visual Documentary,* Dave Thompson/Jo-Ann Greene, Omnibus Press, 1993

Hearings, Committee on Commerce, Science & Transportation, U.S. Senate, September 19, 1985, U.S. Government Printing Office

*Blues Land,* P. Welding, Viking, 1992

*Rock Lives,* Timothy White, Henry Holt, 1990

*Rock of Ages,* Timothy White, Rolling Stone/Summit Books, 1986

*BITCH BITCH BITCH,* Mike Wren, Omnibus Press, 1988

## other:

Liner notes to *Love Gets Strange,* Rhino Records

"Nightline," ABC-TV

# index

# about the authors

Joe Kohut is the author of *So Sue Me!* (Black Tooth Press) and *The Little Book of Phobias* (Running Press). He has worked as a business reporter and editor, and in the late seventies tried to make a living booking bands in Philadelphia. He currently resides in "Everybody's Home Town," Media, Pennsylvania, with his loyal and personable mirth hound E. "Buzz" Kohut. The "E" stands for Elvis.

John J. Kohut is the co-author of five other books, including *Countdown to the Millennium* and *News from the Fringe* (Plume), both with Roland Sweet. John's column, "Countdown to the Millennium," appears in the 'zine *Maximum Rock & Roll*. He lives in Washington, D.C., where he daily guards his spot in line at Ticketron in preparation for the next Springsteen tour.

By the way, it's pronounced Kó-hut.